Ullrich Müller

Black Gold, Black Swans

The importance of the unexpected
for the future of energy

Anchor Compact

Müller, Ullrich: Black Gold, Black Swans: The importance of the unexpected for the future of energy. Hamburg, Anchor Academic Publishing 2013
Original title of the thesis: Oil, electricity and Taleb's ‚Black Swan'

Buch-ISBN: 978-3-95489-085-9
PDF-eBook-ISBN: 978-3-95489-585-4
Druck/Herstellung: Anchor Academic Publishing, Hamburg, 2013
Additionally: Corvinus School of Management Ungarn. Master Thesis, 2012

Bibliografische Information der Deutschen Nationalbibliothek:
Die Deutsche Nationalbibliothek verzeichnet diese Publikation in der Deutschen Nationalbibliografie; detaillierte bibliografische Daten sind im Internet über http://dnb.d-nb.de abrufbar

Bibliographical Information of the German National Library:
The German National Library lists this publication in the German National Bibliography. Detailed bibliographic data can be found at: http://dnb.d-nb.de

© Anchor Academic Publishing, ein Imprint der Diplomica® Verlag GmbH
http://www.diplom.de, Hamburg 2013
Printed in Germany

List of Contents

1. Introduction

"[...] there are known knowns; there are things we know we know. We also know there are known unknowns; that is to say we know there are some things we do not know. But there are also unknown unknowns - the ones we don't know we don't know." (Donald Henry Rumsfeld)[1]

The world is hungry for energy. While old powers seek for untapped sources, newcomers are prepared to play the great game with new vigor, changing the global landscape of energy forever. With the words of Daniel Yergin, one of the foremost experts on the matter, energy has become 'The Quest' of the 21st century.[2] Enormous amounts of capital and human effort are invested into resource exploration, energy generation and transmission, reflecting the insatiable thirst of our growing civilizations. The energy industry and the whole socio-economic system that depends on it are of immense size and importance today and most likely will be even more so in the future. Hence, a stable and reliable flow of cheap and easily accessible energy is an important precondition for further human and economic develop-ment and the increased individual and political safety and stability that comes with it. And yet, history shows that the development of the modern energy fueled global economy was full of unpredictable turns and surprises, often resulting in great human and financial losses.

Thus, this paper does not deal too much with the new world of energy, but rather with some of the risks that come with it. To be more precise, it is about a phenomenon called the 'Black Swan' and its impact on the energy related business. While we shall define later in more detail what a 'Black Swan' actually is, for now, suffice it to say, that in its negative form it is a rare event that hits unexpectedly and causes great damage to everything affected. Its impact is, therefore, enormous and yet it is almost impossible to predict: The 'Black Swan' is the intellectual incarnation of the rare, the unforeseen and the inexplicable. While the ancients called it fate or fortune, in modern times, we often perceive it as bad luck or a lack of knowledge and preparation. We refuse to give it much of a thought. And yet, if we are to

---

[1] Original quote of Donald Rumsfeld, taken from the transcript of a press conference in 2002: DoD News Briefing - Secretary Rumsfeld and Gen. Myers, 12.02.2002,
http://www.defense.gov/transcripts/transcript.aspx?transcriptid=2636, as of 29.07.2012, 02:31.
[2] Yergin used that term as the title of his well-received account on the status quo and the future of energy: Yergin, Daniel: The Quest – Energy, Security, and the Remaking of the Modern World, Allen Lane, London, 2011.

1

secure the protection needed to keep our energy based society stable, we have to make some sense out of the phenomenon, even though it might not fit into theoretic models or mathematical formulas. Therefore, the aim of this paper is to provide a basic problem analysis. The findings, by the nature of the subject, will not be specific, but should translate into some broad insights and recommendations that could be of interest to many different actors in the energy business, be they companies, regulators or private persons alike.

Hence, based on the work of Nassim Nicholas Taleb, we shall first define the concept of the 'Black Swan'. Subsequently, after a critical examination of the strategic prediction models used in the energy business today, the paper will focus on historic data and experiences in order to review to what extent the 'Black Swan' influenced the development of the energy world in the past. In order to apply the necessary methodological rigor, 'Black Swans' and their impact will be measured according to predefined criteria and indicators, which will be elaborated in the first part of the paper. Finally, we shall investigate whether it is possible to draw any practical conclusions for the future, ultimately looking for methods, which could render us capable of taming the 'Black Swan'.

2. Methodological framework and definitions

2.1 The 'Black Swan' – a concept and its application

The concept of the 'Black Swan' has been made popular by Nassim Nicholas Taleb, who in 2007 published a book by that same name.[3] The term itself goes back to the historic fact, that biologists were convinced that there was no such thing as a black swan, until they were taught otherwise by finding one in newly discovered Australia. Taleb uses the metaphor to give a common name to what he defines as high impact events that are deemed so unlikely that they are not considered to be possible, just until they actually happen. In a broader sense, a 'Black Swan' is a phenomenon that hits completely unexpectedly but has a game changing effect. This effect can be positive or negative, but it will definitely put an end to the status quo. However, Taleb's point is not just that unexpected things do happen. Instead he argues that we are actually ignoring them to the point of denial, due to the way our minds are formed. According to Taleb, whenever we make plans for the future, we tend to focus on the foreseeable and base our assumptions on experiences from the past. Thereby we tunnel our thinking by limiting our imagination to history, again neglecting the fundamental role of 'Black Swans' for our lives. At the same time, Taleb elaborates, we are constantly underestimating the power of randomness. Instead of random events, our mind identifies 'anomalies' or 'irregularities'.[4] Even when confronted with the logically inexplicable, we still try to include it into a consistent narrative, which puts the unexpected into a seemingly reasonable context, enabling us to ignore it again. Differently put, our predictions about the future are based on bell-curve type probability models and historic narratives. According to Taleb's argumentation, the problem with that is not only that it makes us blind for randomness, but also that the unexpected can shape our fortune just as much as the expected and predictable. To give an easy example: When we observe a skillful football player, for instance, we assume that his career must be based on talent and hard training. We completely ignore that it was just as important for his professional development, that he never experienced any bad injuries, which might have disabled him to play football ever again. At the same time, there might be dozens of even harder working and more talented players, who just

---

[3] Taleb, Nassim Nicholas: The Black Swan: The Impact of the Highly Improbable, Penguin Books, New York, 2008. The first publication was issued in 2007 in the USA by Random House.

[4] Taleb came to this conclusion already in his earlier work: Taleb, Nassim Nicholas: Fooled by Randomness – The Hidden Role of Chance in Life and in the Markets, Penguin Books, New York, 2007, page xli (prologue). The first edition of the book was published by Random House in the USA in 2005.

happened to get injured and now have to follow a career as accountants or journalists. Hence, their possible impact on the world of sports will never be part of the equation. This is what Taleb calls 'silent evidence'[5] and he argues that we constantly ignore it, due to the so called 'survivor bias'[6]. This bias makes us incur conclusions about success by only looking at the small sample of 'winners', instead of seeing the whole picture of all the promising young boys, who ever dreamed about being professional football players.

But why are we so strongly biased in favor of the seemingly predictable? In order to explain this, Taleb categorizes events into two different types. In his view, they either belong to the realms of what he calls 'Mediocristan' or 'Extremistan'. Whereas in 'Mediocristan' the probability of a certain event or phenomenon indeed follows the normal distribution of the Gaussian bell curve, in 'Extremistan' "wild randomness"[7] is the rule. Since in 'Mediocristan' variability is limited, one has to cope only with mild randomness. In effect, within certain limits, things become predictable. To use one of Taleb's examples: On the one hand, a baker selling his bread can expect profits only within certain limits, related to the number of breads he can produce and sell. Writers and singers, on the other hand, might either starve or become multi-millionaires like Joan K. Rowling or Madonna. Since the human mind is used to process 'Mediocristan' style events, it blurs the distinction between the two realms and consequently applies the wrong rules. Therefore, we assume things to be predictable within given limits, even when they are not. This leads - time and again - to gross miscalculations.

The historic literature is full of examples: From IBM's Thomas Watson, who in 1943 famously predicted a computer world market size of about five pieces[8], over Neville Chamberlain, who proclaimed 'Peace for our time' after signing the Munich Accord just one year before the start of the Second World War[9], to the famous economist Irving Fisher, who on the verge of

---

[5] Taleb: The Black Swan, p. 50.
[6] The best explanation for this concept is delivered in: Taleb: Fooled by randomness, p. 93 and following.
[7] Taleb: The Black Swan, pp. 215-228.
[8] It is, however, controversial, whether Watson ever really made that statement. There is no recorded evidence and many deem it unlikely altogether. IBM itself thinks that the story about it is based on a misunderstanding; see http://www-03.ibm.com/ibm/history/documents/pdf/faq.pdf, page 26, as of 24.03.2012, 13:03. Nevertheless, it makes sense to mention the statement, as it represents many similar claims that have been made about technological progress during history and which seem to be absurd in retrospect.
[9] The BBC published the text of the original press announcement, made after signing the Munich accord on September 30th 1938 under the following link:
http://news.bbc.co.uk/onthisday/hi/dates/stories/september/30/newsid_3115000/3115476.stm, as of 13.03.2012, 13:12.

the great depression predicted bullish stock markets.[10] What all these cases have in common, is that the oracle was blinded by past experience and the therefrom derived probabilities. Ignoring the possibility of random or, at least, ostensive random events, a historic narrative often becomes the basis for predictive analysis.

Therefore, Taleb argues that the very mistake is to try to predict anything specific at all. Since it is impossible to attach a numeric probability to 'Extremistan' events, it is beyond our power to decide on and weight the factors to be put into the equation of any predictive analysis. Furthermore, the possibility of random events strongly inhibits any attempt to get clear predictions of the inductive type, since there is always the possibility that they will be falsified in the future. But if it is impossible to come up with a couple of likely scenarios, how could anybody cope with the risk of taking decisions at all? After all, according to recent research, in everyday life human emotions are an effective decision-making mechanism. With our limited knowledge about complex realities it is impossible to make sophisticated calculations about all kinds of daily decisions. Actually, such calculations would be rather counterproductive. Consequently, habits and emotions become effective short cuts. However, when confronted with more abstract matters, using the human intuition can become rather dangerous, leading to fatal errors.[11]

Rather than trying to prepare for specific situations and conditions, Taleb concludes, we should instead create risk protection through redundancies. He mentions the example of nature, where there are plenty of redundancies, for instance in the human body or in any other biological system.[12] Furthermore, when talking about risk, one should eschew the inductive type of risk measurement and rather apply a Popper-inspired falsifying approach. One should refrain from trying to calculate the probability of risky events, based on historical experiences. Rather one should develop hypothesis about every possible kind of extreme, if unlikely, risk exposure and then try to minimize it.[13] But what is important for now is the question, whether we can find empirical evidence for the 'Black Swan' at work also in the development of the energy business.

---

[10] He even kept sticking to that believe, after the events following the Black Friday had wept out most of his personal capital. For more details: Nasar, Sylvia: Grand Pursuit – The Story of Economic Genius, Simon&Schuster, New York, 2011, p. 312.

[11] Taleb: Fooled by Randomness, p. 182 and following.

[12] Taleb: The Black Swan, p. 312.

[13] Taleb: Fooled by Randomness, p. 120 and following.

But before taking further up on that thought, we still have to consider some important details. First of all, not every high impact event also is a 'Black Swan'. Would, for instance, Israel execute a preemptive air strike against Iran tomorrow, this would certainly have a powerful impact on world politics and economics. However, it would lack the element of random surprise, which is inherent to what we commonly call 'chance' or 'fortune' and which constitutes the 'Black Swan'. Because such an airstrike is a currently discussed possibility, no foreign policy maker would completely rule it out. Consequently, Taleb argues that not even the financial crisis from 2007 should count as a 'Black Swan', since many of its causes and effects were indeed foreseeable and certainly were expected by many in the financial sector.[14] On the other hand, events like the Tsunami in South-East-Asia in 2004 or the one of 2011, which hit alongside earthquakes and a nuclear accident, were certainly impossible to anticipate in their concrete form and magnitude. Therefore, 'Black Swans' are events that not only have a high impact on the most important subsystems of any systemic structure but also run counter scientifically or intuitively perceived probabilities. They might be part of scenario analysis, science fiction movies or described by obscure experts before-hand, however, they will be deemed to be extremely unlikely or even absurd until they happen. Just like with the lottery, particularly rational observers will argue that the probabil-ity of hitting the jackpot is so low, that participation is of no use. However, the extremely high impact of actually winning makes participating still attractive. Once successful, winners will easily accept narratives, explaining why they were bound to be the lucky ones.[15] This explains why often after some high impact event took place, one will find 'historic' lost opportunities for possible in-advance discovery. For instance, in the case of the events of 9/11, the authorities had to face critique for not sharing and ignoring known facts about the to-be terrorists.[16] However, since by the time things actually happened an event loses its a priori unlikeliness, former obscure hints will by then fit into the story as well established facts, like the foolishness of building a nuclear power plant just next to the sea or letting

---

[14] Although of course, nobody was able to exactly foresee what would happen, many actors in the financial markets were aware, that a financial breakdown would be eventually unavoidable. A good account on how the main actors in the financial industry perceived the prelude of the crisis can be found in: Sorkin, Andrew Ross: Too Big To Fail, Penguin Books, New York, 2009. Furthermore, Taleb himself describes the dynamic of market crisis and investor behavior in his book „Fooled by Randomness", which he published already in 2004.

[15] For example, always sticking to the same numbers, never losing hope or just being inspired by a mystical appearance.

[16] A major example for this is of course 'The 9/11 Commission Report', which sharply criticized several government agencies for their failure to cooperate and read the evidence. A freely accessible version of the report is available under: http://www.gpo.gov/fdsys/pkg/GPO-911REPORT/pdf/GPO-911REPORT.pdf, as of 24.03.2012, 13:48.

strangely behaving Arab men learn how to fly an airplane. But this is ex-post-facto-thinking. Even though an event could theoretically have been anticipated, its perceived extreme unlikeliness held it out of the focus and rendered it pure randomness from the point of view of the failed anticipator. Hence, although 9/11 was of course highly predictably from the terrorist's point of view, for the rest of the world its concrete materialization was purely random in terms of predictability. This is what Taleb describes with the turkey model: The turkey, bred to feed a hungry family, is unaware of his planned sudden death, although his butcher is fully aware of the exact date of his slaughtering.[17]

Illustrating his findings with examples portfolio theory, Taleb argues that in order to achieve extraordinary returns investors should focus on many parallel high risk venture type of investments, instead of trying to balance risk by building a portfolio of already proven businesses. The idea behind this is easily expressed in numerical terms. An investment that yields 5 % return in 90% of the cases and loses 10% in remaining 10% of the cases, is on average less attractive than an investment that yields 500% in 10% of the cases and loses 5% 9 out of 10 times. The small losses made in nine of ten occasions are offset by the rain of cash during the 10th occasion. This idea gains even more momentum when considering that, on the other hand, investments perceived as not very risky can turn into all out losses when exposed to a 'Black Swan'.[18] The point is, that in this paper only events which were suffi-ciently perceived to be unlikely before the fact and thus hit the system from its inherent standpoint completely randomly, will be considered to be 'Black Swans'. Furthermore, by definition, in order to qualify as 'Black Swan', the event has to have had an extremely high impact on the system under examination. Therefore, the criteria which constitute a 'Black Swan' are highly relative with regard to the respective party or system under scrutiny.

It is evident at this point, that the proposed criteria for the identification of 'Black Swans' are hardly quantifiable in precise numbers, which makes them hard to measure against any kind of quantitative scale. Fortunately though, Taleb listed them in a summarizing article in the New York Times. A 'Black Swan', according to that definition is an event that fulfills the following criteria:

---

[17] Taleb: The Black Swan, p. 40.
[18] That is valid, provided that there is a strong exposure with a high level of leverage, which can immediately wipe out an investor's equity.

"First, it is an outlier, as it lies outside the realm of regular expectations, because nothing in the past can convincingly point to its possibility. Second, it carries an extreme impact. Third, in spite of its outlier status, human nature makes us concoct explanations for its occurrence after the fact, making it explainable and predictable."[19]

These qualitative criteria shall henceforth be the basis for our analysis. They cannot be measured precisely; however, there are signals that can be used instead. While ex ante improbability has to be proven for each single case according to the historic evidence available, the power of impact can be gauged by some robust indicators that are inter-subjectively verifiable. Since the subject of this paper is energy, oil and electricity prices seem to be suitable for that role. In the next paragraph we shall further discuss this possibility.

2.2. How to measure 'Black Swan' impact - energy prices as an indicator

By energy we henceforth mean oil and electricity and the scope of our examination will be limited to roughly the period starting from the aftermath of WWII. This makes sense in so far, as the current framework of world affairs and economics was largely fixed by the results of that war and has not been changed fundamentally ever since. The boom in the western world following the war was fueled by oil and electricity and the global economy became largely depended on them. Patterns of trade and reliable markets emerged, resulting in global commodity prices. We ought to use this to the advantage of our investigation.

After all, if we are going to search for the 'Black Swan', a common variable regarding the examined system is needed. Let us recall: Taleb proposed three elements that constitute the 'Black Swan': "[...] rarity, extreme impact, and retrospective (though not prospective) predictability [...]".[20] As a counter balance to the historic narrative, which – we remember – is usually quite misleading but delivers a retrospective explanation, we need an empirical indicator that allows us to identify sudden shocks to the system. These shocks would indicate an extreme impact and at the same time allow us to separate the usual from the rare. Consequently, the best indictor in the given field of interest of this paper seem to be the market prices for crude oil and electricity, which shall be used as a proxy, helping to

---

[19] http://www.nytimes.com/2007/04/22/books/chapters/0422-1st-tale.html?_r=1, as of 10.04.2012, 22:10.
[20] Talib, Nassim Nicholas: The Black Swan: The Impact of the highly Improbable, The New York Times, 22.04.2007, http://www.nytimes.com/2007/04/22/books/chapters/0422-1st-tale.html?ex=1178769600&en=bdae1078f2b4a98c&ei=5070, as of 10.04.2012, 22:35.

identify 'Black Swans', alongside the qualitative analysis. Changes, be they gradually or abrupt, are reflected by the prices, which mirror the relevant market developments and reflect external shocks. Finally, it is relatively easy to retrieve the widely available price data and to put it into a common framework. This makes energy prices a reliable and robust indicator that allows us to make comparisons and will underpin the qualitative examination.

Now, if we are going to use energy prices as an empirical 'Black Swans' indicator, it is important to first understand how they arise and were they apply. In contrast to electricity, which is a highly perishable and hardly storable good, there has been a world market for crude oil and it's derivatives already for a long time. Because oil is usually produced far from the place of its usage, by definition the market for oil is an international one, involving different regions through all the steps of the value chain. The US Energy Information Administration consequently defines the oil price as the sum of costs and market conditions.[21] This means, that the price accounts for the production, processing and transportation costs. Depending on the circumstances, they can slightly vary, but are nevertheless the fixed part of the price. Secondly, depending on the market environment, there is a varying premium on the price, which is basically determined by the real or perceived balance between supply and demand. Theoretically, if demand is high, prices should be high too, whereas excessive supply should result in lower prices. Although this is generally true, the vital role of oil for the global economy makes its perceived future supply and demand a matter of much speculation, heavily depending on many indirect factors. Political crisis, natural disasters or economic turmoil can all influence the anticipated future development of the oil market and have a strong influence on the price, sometimes ignoring the real developments. Not least, interventions by the OPEC-cartel - mainly through production quotas - have a decisive influence on the oil price, often limiting the role of the free market in price making. Certainly, it is the OPEC's intention to keep prices on a stable high level. However, it has also shown in the past, that it can play an important in price shock mitigation by providing additional supply in times of crisis. After all, most of its members today have a big stake in the global economy and its general well-being.

---

[21] Office of Oil and Gas, Energy Information Administration: Oil Market Basics, chapter: Prices, http://www.eia.gov/pub/oil_gas/petroleum/analysis_publications/oil_market_basics/price_text.htm, as of 01.04.2012, 13:53.

Finally, since the price development comprises such complex calculations and is bound to vary strongly over time, there is a lot of room for financial speculation. This further aggravates the need for many market players to acquire volatility protection via complicated market instruments. As a result, transactions happen in many different forms, from long term contracts over future trades to the local spot markets. These spot markets are usually the most sensitive indicators of price development because of the immediacy of transactions. In addition, each country charges a different amount of taxes on petrol products, which many times even exceeds the actual market price. This makes taxes one of the single largest determinants of the price. However, for this analysis neither the imposed taxes nor the actual, long term planning based production costs are of any particular interest, since they are relatively fixed and largely predictable. Instead, it is the market condition premium which ought to be in the center of the examination. Here lies the focal point of speculation and here is where the 'Black Swan' can hit the hardest, immediately translating into different prices on the spot market.

Electricity prices on the other hand, depend to a much larger degree on local market conditions. Since electricity cannot be stored or transported effectively over very long distances, markets are necessarily confined to the region of its production. Therefore, prices can strongly vary in different markets. Whereas, for instance, one Kilowatt-hour of electricity in Hungary in 2008 cost on average 0.224 USD, the same Kilowatt-hour in the United States cost in the same year on average 0.113 USD and 0.171 USD in Brazil.[22] To what extent local conditions can determine the price, was exemplified by the California energy crisis at the beginning of the last decade: An ill-conceived liberalization attempt lead to extreme price volatility on the wholesale market, resulting in excessive state debt and finally also high consumer prices. One of the major problems was that - partly due to speculation, partly due to a lack of investment - the supply side did not deliver as expected. Finally even blackouts were the result. Ultimately the ruling Democrats were removed from power and the world marveled at the rise of 'Governator' Arnold Schwarzenegger.[23] In contrast to the oil market, where suppliers can be chosen on a more international level, the local electricity buyers were not able to quickly switch to alternative sources of supply and therefore prices rose

---

[22] According to data published by the EIA in 2010, http://www.eia.gov/emeu/international/elecprih.html, as of 01.04.2012, 21:31. The price for the USA still excludes tax, since it is charged regionally.
[23] A good overview about the course of the crisis can be found in: Yergin, Daniel: The Quest, pp. 379-395. More specialized accounts will be cited later on.

starkly over the level of other regional markets. Due to its high relevance for our topic, we will return later to this case in much more detail.

Another factor, determining the electricity price, is the energy mix used in a given grid system. It might either dependent on prices of primary resource, like with coal, gas or oil, or on political circumstances like in the case of nuclear energy. In other setups even natural conditions may have an influence, as for instance in the case of alternative energy. Since many different technologies are applied to produce electricity, also a wide range of different cost structures and risks are involved. Consequently, electricity markets are much more decentralized than the oil market and face a different set of challenges. However, it needs to be said, that most of the electricity produced today, still comes from the fossil fuels coal, gas and oil. Although many experts see natural gas as the future of that part of the business, most of the industry still depends on coal. In comparison, oil is of less importance, also because many market players anticipate higher prices and, therefore, invest into alterna- tives. Thus, most of the competition unfolds between coal and gas, the former being cheap and easily accessible, the latter promising to become a much cleaner alternative. Further- more, whereas oil is strongly affected by geopolitical risks, coal and gas seem to be a much safer choice for some, since many consumer countries are producers as well. For instance, in the United States the speedy development of the shale gas industry, based on the techno- logical revolution in 'Fracking' technology, has been astonishing, rising from share of about 1% of US gas production in 2000 to 25% a decade later. But consumption and production of coal and gas also create significant environmental risks: From water pollution and earth- quakes, possibly caused by 'Fracking', to the massive emission of CO_2 by burning huge amounts of coal. [24] Therefore, renewables are expected to take over an ever increasing share in the energy mix. However, at the moment most of the developing technologies still cannot compete on price with the existing sources. For that reason, many observers - especially in the developing world – still see nuclear energy as a carbon free and cheap alternative to conventional sources, despite the risk of devastating accidents. In sum, electricity is a very flexible form of energy, which can be produced in many ways and from a lot of different resources. But it is hard to store, highly perishable and as a result confined to regional markets. Oil is easy to store and transport, making it a global commodity. However, its

---

[24] Data and facts in above paragraph were taken from: http://www.economist.com/node/21540275, The Economist, Nov 26th 2011.

production is limited to a few sources, which can be easily monopolized. Hence, prices in both areas have their own determinants and dynamics. When it comes to 'Black Swan' type risk, one would thus expect different levels and layers of exposure - a topic to which we shall certainly return later on in this paper.

2.3. A critique of Energy outlooks – predictions in the light of 'Black Swans'

Having discussed earlier how difficult it is to make predictions about the future that hold against reality, we ought to take a look now on how players in the energy business try to do it. A traditionally published, major instrument is the energy outlooks, which many institutions and companies in and around the business issue on a regular basis. Usually these documents aim on predicting long term development trends by using driver based models. The utilized drivers are mainly based on historical and present trends and the therefrom derived probabilities. This causes them to suffer from what Taleb calls a 'confirmation bias'. That means that an analyst deems a predicted outcome the more likely the more 'historical evidence' he can collect to assist his hypothesis, even though the lack of counter evidence over a long period of time make its final appearance actually more likely.[25] In consequence, these models usually ignore the possibility of random events, may they be great leaps in technological development or natural catastrophes alike and focus instead on narratives, like for example the rise of China and India or the quest for alternative energy. For instance, in its "2012 The Outlook for Energy: A View to 2040", the oil and gas producer ExxonMobil regards world population growth, demographic trends and the process of maturing of economies in the developing world to a higher living standard as drivers for a postulated increase in global energy demand of about 30% until 2040, including a slowdown supposed to start around the year 2025. According to the report, the biggest chunk of that demand should come from electricity production, which should by then account for about 40% of the overall energy demand.[26] Malcolm Brinded, the Executive-Director-Upstream-International of Shell, predicted in a speech at the FT Global Energy Leaders' Summit in London in June

---

[25] Taleb explains this point, using natural evolution as a background: The longer a given species succeeds in surviving, the more likely observers are to incur, that it must be the species' superior qualities that make it survive for so long. However, fitness to survive is always linked to a specific set of circumstances and the more a species adapts to them over time, the more likely its eventual extinction becomes, once the circumstances change. Thus, there is also a 'survivor bias', Taleb, Fooled by Randomness, p. 96.

[26] "2012 The Outlook for Energy: A View to 2040",
http://www.exxonmobil.com/Corporate/Files/news_pub_eo2012.pdf, as of 31.03.2012, 13:23, page 1-6.

2011 that energy demand might double or even triple until 2050, "[...] if emerging econo-mies follow historical patterns of development."[27] Brinded also sees population growth and the rise of the developing world as key drivers. Although he believes in a strong increase in alternative energies, he is nevertheless confident, that in 2050 still 60% of the energy demand will be covered by fossil fuels. Despite his demand side optimism, Brinded also warns, that on the supply side heavy investments will be needed to match the demand.[28] In order to manage price volatility in the sensitive transport sector, Brinded proposes the increased use of bio fuels like ethanol and LNG, as a substitute for Diesel.[29]   BP on the other hand, predicts a 39% growth in energy demand until 2030, identifying popula-tion and income growth, expressed by rising GDPs, as the main drivers.[30] BP as well sees the bulk of the growth coming from the developing world, while, according to their prediction, the consumption levels of the OECD states will remain flat.[31]

The general notion behind the energy outlook prediction efforts is summed up nicely once more by what IEA Chief Economist Fatih Birol said in an interview in March 2012: He identi-fied "[...] in particular increasing car ownership in China, India and the Middle East as a driver of the new demand.".[32] Birol used these drivers in order to describe the demand side, which he sees to be following an upwards movement. On the other hand, he cautioned observers not to be too optimistic about the ability of the supply side to deliver on the increasing demand, because the " [...] significant reserves of oil underground [...] do not immediately translate into greater supply at filling stations.".[33]

It is safe to say, that this model – a quick and steady increase on the demand side, driven mainly by the growth in the developing world with a somewhat lower increase on the supply side and mitigated by the worldwide quest to increase energy efficiency – is close to consen-

---

[27] Malcolm Brinded: Global Energy Outlook and Policy Implications, http://www-static.shell.com/static/media/downloads/speeches/brinded_london_28062011a.pdf, as of 31.03.2012, 14:24, page 3.
[28] Brinded: Global Energy Outlook, p. 3.
[29] Brinded: Global Energy Outlook, p. 7.
[30] BP Energy Outlook 2030, London, January 2012, http://www.bp.com/liveassets/bp_internet/globalbp/STAGING/global_assets/downloads/O/2012_2030_energy_outlook_booklet.pdf, as of 31.03.2012, 14:59.
[31] BP Energy Outlook 2030, p. 10.
[32] The remarks were made in an Interview on the BBC's 'Business Daily" show, transcribed on the website of the IEA: http://www.iea.org/journalists/index.asp, as of 23.03.2012, 15:32. The link to the original televised interview is: http://www.bbc.co.uk/iplayer/episode/p00pfhq5/Business_Daily_Back_to_the_future/, as of 23.03.2012, 15:33.
[33] http://www.iea.org/journalists/index.asp, as of 23.03.2012, 15:32.

sus among industry experts compiling their energy outlooks. The implicit conclusion of all these models clearly is that oil prices will soar during the coming decades. The rationale behind this hypothesis is, that while demand for fossil fuels will further increase, the supply side will be immensely challenged trying to deliver. This notion is so strongly reconfirmed by many different sources and analyses - remember the confirmation bias - that the rising prices hypothesis has become something close to common public knowledge. In the public discourse, this is often further substantiated by the widely spread notion of 'peak oil'.[34] Although invoked many times in the past and just as often revised by new reserve findings, 'peak oil' intuitively seems to make sense, since resource depletion is a very basic and plausible human experience. Thus, critics and proponents of the oil business alike, see the oil price on the rise in the future. However, often they seem to ignore, that the drivers they use to form their models are far from being constants. As we learned from the statements cited above, the IEA expects a strong increase in demand. As one of the main drivers behind that increase, the organization identifies high expected growth rates in the transportation sector of the developing world. In fact, the IEA predicts, that until 2035 about 90% of the increase in demand will come from the markets of developing countries like China, India and Brazil.[35] This implies steady economic growth rates in these economies during the next few decades. At the same time it also assumes that there will be no major technological breakthroughs during that period. But in order to be able to treat these factors as a constant base case, also other systems would have to remain stable. Any major political crisis, technological innova-tion or natural catastrophe could potentially change the pre-assumptions of the IEA's prediction. Therefore, any strategy based on such predictions would be heavily exposed to 'Black Swans'. Of course, analysts usually try to factor-in unpredictability by basing their analysis on different scenarios. However, these scenarios only allow for variants of the underlying base case. By their very nature, they cannot account for unpredictable develop-ments. In most of the cases, scenarios are used in the form of having favorable conditions in one scenario standing against unfavorable conditions in another one and finally something in between in a third scenario. They reflect the possible variations of a bell curve type normal distribution, implying also respective probabilities for the average and the outliers. However,

---

[34] An in-depth discussion of the history of the peak oil hypothesis can be found in Daniel Yergin's "The Quest": Yergin: The Quest, pp. 227-241.
[35] WORLD ENERGY OUTLOOK 2011 FACTSHEET
, IEA, http://www.worldenergyoutlook.org/docs/weo2011/factsheets.pdf, 23.03.2012, 23:47, page 1.

this is basically a questionable approach, since it completely ignores unlikely and unforeseeable extreme events, confusing a distribution's median with its average. Thus, in conclusion, the driver based scenario analysis used in the discussed Energy Outlook models can be characterized as an attempt to apply bell-curve-type probability to phenomena within the realm of 'Extremistan'. Following Taleb's analytical framework, the main problem with this kind of approach is that it is basically inductive.[36] As already explained earlier, this means, that predictions are based on data and experiences from the past, which does not account for fallibility. Instead of applying the principles proposed by Karl Popper, which treat assumptions only as working hypotheses, industry analysts - from an epistemological point of view - appear to be rather positivistic.

It seems, therefore, justified to ask whether energy firms that use such analysis, are able to cope with the risks associated with a possible failure to predict future developments. This is especially true for prices, which are crucial factors for most predictive models but are bound to be volatile and therefore impossible to predict in the short term.[37] Even if the high price hypothesis would prove to be true in the future, that does not mean that there will be no unexpected and sudden price changes in the meantime. Thus, even if the Energy outlooks predictions would be accurate for the year 2035, that does not automatically mean, that the world would see a steady price increase until then. Rather, there could be sudden price jumps all along the way. On average, they might level out and confirm the strategist's predictions, but nevertheless they could be sufficient at any given point in time to wipe out entire businesses and a lot of capital.[38] Again, the overall result of a trend based analysis, trying to account for events within the next 20 to 30 years, might at the end prove to be just outright wrong. To give a tangible example for the fallibility of price predictions: While currently many integrated oil firms prosper, thanks to huge windfalls from unexpectedly high returns on their long term development and exploration projects, which are mainly due to lower price predictions at the time these projects were budgeted, exactly the opposite happened to the OPEC-countries in the 1990s: Just after they had agreed on higher output levels, prices plummeted due to the Russian and the Asian crisis and left the oil producing

---

[36] Taleb: Fooled by Randomness, p. 120 and following.

[37] Taleb explains the mathematical problem behind that problem in Fooled by Randomness. While volatility levels out over a long term time scale, on a very short term time scale, like for example one minute or even one hour, it creates so much noise, that it is impossible to derive any conclusions from such temporary data. Taleb, Fooled by Randomness, pp. 64-69.

[38] Taleb: Fooled by Randomness, pp. 64-69.

countries which huge revenue losses, if compared to their expectations.[39] As a result, many companies today try to focus on the upstream part of the business, while refining, which saw a golden age beforehand, has become unattractive and the actual consumer sales in the Retail sector in some cases even produce losses. With all this volatility, is it really wise to link one's strategy to expected future price developments? In order to provide some answers to that question, we shall now move a step back and take a look at the past.

[39] Yergin: The Quest, p. 84 and following.

3. Analysis – The 'Black Swan' in the history of oil and electricity

3.1. Oil – a global commodity in turbulent times

3.1.1 1945-1970 – A phase of stability

The phase between 1945 and 1970 was characterized by relatively stable oil prices, nominally as well as on real price level.[40] In fact, since the mid-19th century, when crude oil was marketed for the first time in history on a larger scale, prices had actually fallen significantly. Low prices coincided with constant economic growth and increasing prosperity in the Western countries, even though, on the political level this period saw a lot of international tension and crisis. However, events like the Berlin Blockade, the Korean War or the Cuba Crisis, which all happened against the background of the unfolding Cold War between the two Superpowers USA and USSR, failed to have a decisively harmful effect on energy production and resource availability. Hopes for further technical development were high, especially in the field of nuclear energy and it is therefore characteristic, that the only true shocks the oil dependent system saw in the period between the World Wars and the 1970s - the Iran coup and the Suez crisis - led to a boom in the nuclear energy business, symbolized by France's quest for nuclear fuel energy autarky under De Gaulle and Pompidou.[41] Despite that, throughout the described period, oil was cheaply available, thanks to the increasing production from the new world oil power Saudi Arabia and the exploitation of other newly discovered sources. In compliance with what we concluded in the previous chapter, stable conditions created an increasingly high exposure to game changing events. Businesses didn't plan for significant oil shortages. Consumers drove large cars with inefficient engines and no Western politician would have made energy diversification an election campaign topic. In sum, history saw an unprecedented economic boom, fueled by oil and undisturbed by excessive volatility. Clearly, this description fits the turkey model introduced by Taleb: Each day of security fuels the confirmation bias, which fools the observer and creates the false impression of eternal progress and reliability. Only a completely unexpected game changing event could alter this situation. And exactly such an event happened in the fall of 1973 and shook the whole oil depended system, from consumers, industry and governments to the major oil companies.

---

[40] All oil price references, if not stated otherwise, are taken from table 1 and table 2 in the Appendix and will, therefore, not be further referenced.
[41] Yergin: The Quest, pp. 374-375.

3.1.2. The oil shock and how it changed the world

On the 6th of October 1973 Egypt and Syria launched a surprise attack on territories held by Israel in the Sinai and on the Golan Heights. The unfolding war, which was subsequently named the Yom Kippur war, resulted in an unprecedented embargo of Middle Eastern oil producing states against the industrialized West. Since these states supported the attacks on Israel, for the first time in history they used the 'oil weapon' against Israel's Western allies in order to force them to cease their support for the Jewish state. The immediate effect was a dramatic increase of the crude oil price, which amounted to about 70% within just a couple of days. Skyrocketing prices finally resulted in an economic recession in the West and fueled a general feeling of crisis and decline. Not only did the crisis harm businesses, it also reflected on private consumers. Many countries introduced traffic volume limitations on certain days and ran energy efficiency campaigns. The oil shortages arrived at such concerning levels, that the United States even made concrete plans to cease the Oil producing facilities in Saudi Arabia, Kuwait und Abu Dhabi militarily, as recently declassified British government documents revealed.[42] Many governments now were forced to acknowledge the need for change if they were to maintain their country's energy security.

The oil crisis revealed the strong dependence of the developed world on a steady and cheap flow of oil, making it the Achilles heel of the West and a strong weapon for the oil producing countries. Organizing themselves in the OPEC, which became effectively the ruling mechanism of a producer price cartel, these formerly rather weak and internationally unimportant states were suddenly able to command a considerable amount of political leverage.[43]

Hence, applying the theoretic framework of what constitutes a 'Black Swan', we have already established via the oil price indicator, that the oil crisis of 1973 was definitely an extreme impact event, since it completely broke out of the scale of earlier price peaks, both in altitude and in velocity. As for the first time in history the 'oil weapon was applied, having a game changing effect on the international political system, it is fair to also call it sufficiently rare. But was it also really unpredictable from a contemporary observer's point of view? At this point, it seems that we are confronted again with the turkey model problem: While the

---

[42] Further details on these plans can be found in a BBC online article, written by Paul Reynolds in 2004. http://news.bbc.co.uk/2/hi/middle_east/3333995.stm, as of 07.04.2012, 18:42.

[43] Above paragraph is based on: Yergin, Daniel: The Prize – The Epic Quest for Oil, Money & Power, The Free Press, New York, 1991, pp. 588-612 and Campanini, Massimo: Storia del Medio Oriente 1798 – 2006, Il Mulino, Bologna, 2007, pp. 125-158.

war and perhaps even the oil embargo was highly predictable from the perpetrators perspective, for the rest of the world the Yom Kippur war was a complete surprise and not the result of rising tensions or a diplomatic stalemate. In fact, it was the element of surprise the made waging the war so attractive for Egypt and Syria in the first place. While Jewish Israelis where celebrating the holy Yom Kippur, the attackers found Israel's defense forces unprepared and off the guard. Israel came close to a defeat, which was only avoided because to the first time, the US really committed itself strongly to the defense of the Jewish state. They organized an immediate air lift, delivering weapons, supplies and ammunition.[44] In direct consequence of the war, which was certainly a psychological victory for the Arabs, the - until then successful - Israeli Prime Minister Golda Meir had to resign. On the long term the perceived defeat of 1973 lead to the rise of the right wing Likud party and caused an increasing polarization within the Israeli society. In the West, the Arab use of the oil weapon had certainly not been anticipated. The Middle Eastern oil had been regarded as an alternative to a premature exploitation of home based sources and not much effort was put into increasing energy efficiency. This quickly changed: The Nixon government, like every US government ever since, publically declared the need to diversify the nation's energy supply and committed to an energy austerity program, urging US-citizens to refrain from excessive and unnecessary use of oil and gas and taking concrete actions in order to drive down the energy demand. Instead of relying on foreign suppliers, Nixon warned, "Our independence will depend on maintaining and achieving self-sufficiency in energy [...]"[45]. The legislative result of Nixon's efforts was the 1973 Emergency Petroleum Allocation Act, which aimed on giving price incentive for increasing oil production and fuel efficiency and established the Strategic Petroleum Reserve.[46] Furthermore, on the public policy front Nixon initiated the so called 'Project Independence 1980'. The aim was "[...] to not have to rely on any source of energy beyond our own [...]"[47] by 1980. Both - Nixon's somewhat futile attempts to quickly fix a strategic problem and Golda Meir's demise - are symptoms for the fact, that although the

---

[44] The sensitive negotiations and consideration that led to the strong commitment of the USA are well described in: Dallek, Robert: Nixon and Kissinger: Partner in Power, HarperCollins, New York, 2007, chapter 12, p. 369 and following.

[45] Richard Nixon: "Address to the Nation About National Energy Policy.", November 25, 1973. Online by Gerhard Peters and John T. Woolley, The American Presidency Project.
http://www.presidency.ucsb.edu/ws/index.php?pid=4051#axzz1rfyvqWkz, as of 10.04.2012, 23:52.
[46]http://www.eia.gov/pub/oil_gas/petroleum/analysis_publications/chronology/petroleumchronology2000.htm#T_4_, as of 11.04.2012, 23:04.
[47] Richard Nixon: "Address to the Nation About National Energy Policy.," November 25, 1973. Online by Gerhard Peters and John T. Woolley, The American Presidency Project.

Yom Kippur war and the following embargo were impossible to predict from ex ante, contemporaries felt, that both should and could have been foreseen. Hence, Meir had to resign for her failure to do so and Nixon tried to atone by rushing into an energy version of the quest to the moon. However, the retrospectively astonishing fact, that until 1973 there was no such thing as the Strategic Petroleum Reserve, which with its - on average – reserves of more than 500 million barrels of crude oil[48] would be able to substitute the daily US-imports for a considerable amount of time, tells a lot about pre-oil-crisis perceptions and expectations. And this is true not just for the USA, but also on an international level. In 1974, about 20 other nations joined the US in their effort to establish strategic oil reserves and founded the International Energy Agency (IEA) in order to coordinate these activities. It currently has 28 member states.[49]

In sum, it is fair to say that the 1973 developments came as a complete surprise to the parties that were affected the most. A fact, which was confirmed in interviews with contemporary political executives like Henry Kissinger, who during that period was US secretary of state and in a filmed interview declared, that the government was completely surprised and literally plan-less. According to Kissinger, all inter-governmental analyses indicated, that the oil price could peak at up to 5.25 USD at the end of the 1970s. However, within a year after those analyses were made, it reached levels above 15 USD.[50] The crisis established the OPEC almost overnight as a credible force in energy and world politics and made many in the Western world realize that something had to be done about the dependency of oil in general and of the Middle Eastern one in particular. For the first time in post-war-history, oil supplies had to be rationed. From an energy industry point of view, 1973 revealed the need for the development of additional crude oil sources and started the quest for more efficiency in production and refining.[51] Alongside increased exports from smaller Middle Eastern states, the oil business increasingly focused on the North Sea offshore exploration and sources in Alaska – with endemic accidents and oil spills in the sea as a consequence. Nevertheless, like

---

[48]http://www.eia.gov/pub/oil_gas/petroleum/analysis_publications/chronology/petroleumchronology2000.htm#T_4_, as of 11.04.2012, 23:04.
[49] http://www.iea.org/about/index.asp, as of 11.04.2012, 23:20.
[50] Kissinger made these claims in an interview, filmed by and published on the website of the IEA: http://www.iea.org/multimedia/videos_info.asp?filename=KISSINGER.flv, as of 11.04.2012, 23:46, starting from 0:44 minutes.
[51]http://www.eia.gov/pub/oil_gas/petroleum/analysis_publications/chronology/petroleumchronology2000.htm#T_4_, as of 11.04.2012, 23:04.

most states also the USA were unable to stop the trend of growing independency on foreign oil[52], which was bound to keep the world economy exposed to further big scale shocks.

3.1.3. The Iran crisis

The next big shock should come from a country, which in 1973 still had been perceived as an island of calm and stability in an ocean of change and uproar: Persia, the later Iran. Under the rule of the shah, the country positioned itself as a loyal ally of the West and tried to make up for global supply losses resulting from the 1970s embargos. But in late 1978 the situation changed abruptly, as the Iranian revolution caused heavy production losses, which were to remain unchecked until 1981 and produced an all-time-high crude oil price. The prices rose from about 14 USD in 1979 to more than 35 USD in 1981.[53]

Iran already had a long history as an oil producer for the West, going back to the times of the Anglo-Iranian oil company. In 1943 it was already seen as a strategic prey by the big powers of the time, who it hosted during the crucial Teheran conference. Subsequently, with the Mosaddegh-crisis in the late 50s of the last century, it became sufficiently clear, that the Iranian oil was an asset worth fighting for. Back then, pro-Western forces prevailed and the stream of oil continued to flow. But the oil money spurred political ambition, too. The shah tried to establish himself as the heir of the ancient Persian throne and started to gain a higher profile on the international level. Since at that time the influence of the old colonial powers began to fade, a power vacuum emerged in the region - and none of the Western powers had the intention to fill it. Faced with a relative US-decline, the Nixon administration tried to rely rather on friendly regional champions than on its own power and, thus, it came handy, that the shah was willing to take a leading role in the region.[54] However, this ap-proach backfired, when Muhammad Reza suddenly lost his power in 1979. In spite of his increasing international influence and prestige, the shah lost control over internal develop-ments in his country. Ever since the 1950s, his main instrument of power had been authori-tarian repression, which, however, had helped to create a rising hidden opposition. Tired of the secular dictatorship, but mostly driven by increasing economic hardships that were

---

[52]http://www.eia.gov/pub/oil_gas/petroleum/analysis_publications/chronology/petroleumchronology2000.ht m#T_4_, as of 11.04.2012, 23:04.
[53]http://www.eia.gov/pub/oil_gas/petroleum/analysis_publications/chronology/petroleumchronology2000.ht m#T_8_ as of 12.04.2012, 00:06.
[54] For above paragraph consider Yergin: The Prize, pp. 563-566.

aggravating during the second half of the 1970s, people turned to the political Islam and the Mullahs, who became an emerging political force.[55] Yet, when finally millions of people stormed the streets in 1978 and 1979, this came as a surprise to most observers, just as this was the case more recently with the events of the so called Arab spring in 2011. Finally, Ayatollah Khomeini, who had become the iconic revolution leader, could return from exile, while the shah was forced to leave his country forever. The political effect was a complete change of the strategic map of the Middle East, with far reaching consequences until this day. However, with regard to the topic of this paper, the immediate economic impact is of more interest for now. The violent events of 1978 and 1979 and the radical, chaos-inducing change of Iran's political landscape in the subsequent years resulted in a massive production loss of about 3.9 million barrels of crude oil per day, which triggered the already mentioned price increases. At its worst point, the political crisis drove output levels down to about 500,000 barrels of crude oil per day – a triviality compared to the almost seven million barrels per day produced in the years before the change. In fact, the output peak in the last years of the Shah-regime should never be reached again after its demise, stabilizing at about 3 to 4 million barrels per day up until today.[56] In addition to this sudden loss of production, many countries tried to increase their stocks and to create stronger buffers, which further aggravated the rise in demand. It did not help either, that the positive economic development in East Asia created even bigger demand pressure. Hence, the higher price levels prevailed throughout the first half of the 1980s, although throughout the period prices were again in a steady decline. The higher price levels allowed producers to finally exploit also minor sources and to go to new lengths in order to acquire new wells. The North Sea oil trend continued forcefully, while also countries like Canada and Mexico became more important crude oil exporters.

Once again, observers at the time had not seen coming what eventually happened. Since the protest of the masses against the shah seemed to reflect the popular will, many western politicians actually supported Khomeini and his revolution. Not only did they grant him exile, but they also actively supported his rise. By urging the shah to open up the political room for protest and thus, for Khomeini, US-president Carter indirectly supported a man, who would

---

[55] Campanini, Storia del Medio Oriente 1798 – 2006, p. 159-161.
[56] A comprehensive price chart regarding Iran's crude oil output can be found on the webpage of WTRG Economics: http://www.wtrg.com/oil_graphs/PAPRPIR.gif, as of 09.05.2012, 22:50. The chart can be found also in the Appendix under table 4.

later call the USA 'the great devil' and initiate a thorough cleansing of the Persian elite, resulting in the creation of an Islamic republic. The dramatic hostage situation in the US-embassy in 1979 was another indirect and unintended consequence. It ultimately even contributed to Carter's replacement by Ronald Reagan in the elections of 1980. Certainly, from Carter's perspective this was an unintended result too. The very fact, that even before his presidency, the US foreign policy saw a Shah-ruled Persia as a center piece of its strategy towards the Middle East, illustrates the fact, that his complete demise was neither anticipated nor actually intended. Furthermore, the unfolding war between Iran and Iraq during the 1980s would have been certainly unthinkable with the shah still in power. In effect, Saddam Hussein of Iraq became a less than perfect strategic substitute. In consequence, he was able to muster support from the US for his fight against the Mullahs - a decision which should ultimately backfire for the Americans and cause another crisis in the region.

Let us apply again our theoretical framework: As the extreme oil price increase shows, the Iranian Revolution with all its aftereffects was certainly an extreme impact event. Since only very few events reshape an entire region's strategic landscape and have a global long term effect, it was without doubt, also sufficiently rare. Finally, as the not very well advised actions of western politicians show, the whole crisis was, especially in its dire consequences, also fairly unpredictable - despite the fact that the mounting tensions within the country were certainly visible. After all, we must remember, that clerics and shopkeepers stood against a mighty police force and a professional military, backed by the enormous revenues from the oil industry. The radical change of Persia from a strategic partner to an anti-Western Islamic republic was simply not on world history's menu before. Hence, also experts failed to predict rising prices. Analyst Dermot Gately, for instance, argued still in October 1979: "In the coming five years [1979-1984] virtually all analyses project a continuation of current market conditions in the world oil market. . . . But we do not expect substantial changes in real prices, down or up, given the stabilizing position of Saudi Arabia and its Arab allies on the Persian Gulf."[57] Nothing could have been further from reality. Once again the 'Black Swan' had fooled all experts.

---

[57] Dermot Gately, "The Prospects for OPEC Five Years after 1973-74," European Economic Review, vol. 12 (October 1979), p. 378.

3.1.4. The 1986 oil price collapse

Apart from events like the 1973 Oil crisis and the Iranian revolution, which resulted in rising oil prices, there were also several unexpected developments that had the opposite effect. One such event was the 1986 oil price collapse. Based on the decision of Saudi Arabia to not act as a swing producer anymore and to link its crude oil prices to the value of refined oil products in order to aggressively increase its market share, many oil producing countries began to increase their output as well, to defend their market share. A downwards price spiral was the certainly unintended consequence: Within half a year, the crude oil price decreased by more than 50%.[58] To be sure, also the years before 1986 saw steady price erosion, amounting to a compound decrease of about 40%. However, the wide use of the so called netback pricing since 1985 and the unilateral production increases of Saudi Arabia really launched an avalanche. Unlike the slow price decrease in the years before, which was mainly based on decreasing demand due to increasing energy efficiency and the reinforced use of alternative energy sources in the consumer countries, the 1986 price collapse happened due to a surprising turn of events. As, for instance, Dermot Gately concludes in his paper about the 1986 price collapse, the sudden price decrease came as a total surprise to everyone. Although Saudi Arabia was the driving force behind the increasingly fierce competition and although it was at first able to almost maintain its former revenues, thanks to the increased sales volume, it also suffered eventually, when prices went further down to the bottom.[59] Thus, it is safe to say, that the 1986 developments came as surprise to all the parties involved, including Saudi Arabia, which originally had planned on increasing its profit share. They certainly had a high impact, if we take the price collapse alone. And since Saudi Arabia's unilateral decision was no less than a paradigm change for the country as well as for OPEC, the crisis can be also characterized as sufficiently rare, in order to qualify as a 'Black Swan'. Since, however, their effect on most of the oil consuming world was actually positive, the events of 1986 did not become a crucial part of the historic narrative. In retrospect, for many observers the year 1986 was also linked much stronger with the Chernobyl accident in the Soviet Union. This terrible incident failed, however, to have a strong influence on the energy markets, since its effect on the energy supply was quite limited. Nevertheless, in the

---

[58] Namely from 23.29 USD in December 1985 to 9.85 USD in July 1986.
http://www.eia.gov/pub/oil_gas/petroleum/analysis_publications/chronology/petroleumchronology2000.htm
#T_10_, as of 30.04.2012, 18:24.
[59] http://www.brookings.edu/~/media/Files/Programs/ES/BPEA/1986_2_bpea_papers/1986b_bpea_gately_ad
elman_griffin.pdf, as of 30.04.2012, 18:48, page 242.

contemporary historic literature it is often seen as a starting point of the even bigger events that should follow only a few years later.[60]

3.1.5. The late 80s, the demise of Communism and the first Gulf Crisis

The period after 1986 certainly saw a fair share of game changing events. The biggest of which was doubtlessly the peaceful dissolution of the USSR and the demise of Communism in the former Eastern Bloc. Regarding the oil business in particular, the Valdez accident in 1989 changed the way in which many big energy firms handled their operations. However, in terms of supply, the impact was minimal and if there was any effect regarding the price development, it was a rather psychological one. More surprisingly, also the monumental historical change caused by the events in the Soviet Union had only a small immediate impact on the oil price. Although certainly of high impact and a surprise to most observers, it apparently did not change the market situation regarding the oil supply, even though on the long term the new possibilities created by the opening of the Eastern economies should have a profound global impact on the crude oil markets.[61] In fact, the production losses due to the political instability in the former Soviet Union were offset by other producers. Much more influential in that regard was a somewhat smaller event that again took place in the Middle East: The Gulf crisis of 1990 which involved some of the biggest oil producers in the world and should result in the first western Gulf War against Saddam Hussein's Iraq.

In August 1990 Iraq's armed forces invaded tiny Kuwait, in order to mark its status as a regional hegemon and to secure the substantial oil reserves in the border region with the Emirate, which it had never recognized as an independent nation anyway. The surprising attack caused global fears of a repetition of the oil crisis of the 1970s and triggered an immediate upwards price spiral. From 16 USD in July 1990, prices rose to 36 USD in September of that same year.[62] Only the successful intervention of UN-forces combined with a release of stock from strategic global oil reserves eased the pressure on the crude oil price and led to a stabilization of price levels in the markets. Not only was Iraq disturbing the balance of peace in the region, by trying to attack various neighboring countries like Israel

---

[60] For example Bernd Stöver, as reflected in: Stöver, Bernd: Der Kalte Krieg 1947 – 1990: Geschichte eines radikalen Zeitalters, Beck, 2007.

[61] A good summary of which can be found in: Yergin, The Quest, pp. 21-82.

[62]http://www.eia.gov/pub/oil_gas/petroleum/analysis_publications/chronology/petroleumchronology2000.htm#T_13_, as of 01.05.2012.

and Saudi Arabia with its Scud missiles. But from the very beginning it became also clear, that oil would play a major role during 'the mother of all battles'. It is therefore, quite symptomatic, that the first prisoners of war during the conflict, were captured on an oil platform off the coast of Kuwait on 19.01.1991.[63] Just a few days later, fleeing Iraqi troops torched Kuwaiti oil wells, producing the great smoke clouds famously covered by the media. The resulting fires were hard to fight and contributed to the increasing fears in the markets, which drove the oil price to new heights. After all, Iraq used the 'oil weapon' not only via the markets but also quite literally: As reports from 24.01.1991 indicate, Saddam's troops apparently caused oil slicks, moving south of Kuwait, with the apparent goal to disturb the Allied fleet's movements. As a result, the Allied forces were forced to bomb Iraqi-held Kuwaiti oil facilities, which further spurred fears of oil supply shortages. Only a couple of days after the oil slicks were discovered, experts estimated the clean-up costs alone to be as high as one billion US-Dollars. Although eventually the damage done by the oil slicks turned out to be smaller than predicted, the almost daily news about the always increasing numbers of burning oil wells – at the end of the war about 600 of the more than 900 Kuwaiti oil wells were burning[64] - and the spread of a crude oil layer on the sea, certainly caused a strong sense of alarm in the general public as well as in the markets. Nevertheless, thanks to the striking military superiority of the Allied forces, the crisis was resolved relatively quickly, once the operations on the ground had started. Hundreds of thousands of Iraqi soldiers lost their lives or were taken prisoners. Saddam's armed forces were quickly eliminated and their equipment was largely destroyed. Iraq's army had to abandon Kuwait and Saddam himself could secure his power only by using chemical weapons against local uprisings because the Allied forces showed a lack of commitment to take over the country. In the aftermath of the war, Iraq became an international outcast, punished with import and export embargos on anything except medicine and food and found itself under constant air control of the UN-forces. Nevertheless, neither were some of the key actors in the US government satisfied with this new state of affairs, nor was Saddam prepared to cut back on his ambitions, however rhetorical they might have been at that point. Eventually this would result in another crisis, the impact of which is felt till this day and will be further discussed later on. At this point, however, we should return to our analysis' framework: Was the 1990 Iraqi

---

[63] The underlying chronology of events used for this chapter was compiled by USA Today: http://www.usatoday.com/news/index/iraq/nirq050.htm, as of 06.05.2012, 11:09.
[64] http://news.bbc.co.uk/2/hi/middle_east/2754103.stm, as of 06.05.2012, 11:31.

invasion of Kuwait a surprise for the major market actors of the time? Given the above mentioned extreme price movements, this seems certainly to be the case: After the Iraqi invasion, prices skyrocketed to the above mentioned levels, only to collapse when it became clear during the first successful US-airstrikes, that the coalition forces would drive home a quick victory.[65] But not only traders and investors were surprised. Also the main political actors did not grasp the dynamic of the crisis beforehand. Although Iraq had never given up on its claims on Kuwait and its oil, few observers expected Saddam to default on its debt towards the Emirate by invading it. This holds true even despite press reports of an increasing Iraqi troop concentration at the border to Kuwait.[66] Only shortly before the invasion, the US ambassador to Iraq told Saddam, that the US had no opinion on inter-Arabian border conflicts like the one between Iraq and Kuwait, implying that Kuwait did not have any defense treaty with the USA[67] – certainly a most careless statement for someone who would expect Saddam to actually start an invasion shortly afterwards. Apparently, the ambassador's remarks should lead the Iraqi president to believe that the US would not interfere. On the other hand, Saddam faced a surprise of his own. Miscalculating political realities of the post-Perestroika global system, a somewhat controllable war against a small neighbor turned out to become 'the mother of all battles'. Instead of easily defeating tiny countries limited forces, Iraq suddenly had to fight against an international coalition led by the militarily far superior US-Americans. Not only had Saddam been unable to foresee that the US would react as strongly as it eventually did. In addition, he had also failed to predict, that the USSR, on the other hand, would actually support an US-led international coalition without much discussion. In sum, Iraq was surprised to find itself internationally isolated, just after fighting an exhausting and costly war against the world's former 'outlaw' Iran. After all, back then it still had gotten plenty of international support. In any event, the whole crisis spurred enormous fears in the markets and let to increased uncertainty among business leaders - not only because the whole affair came as a surprise for everyone despite

---

[65] http://www.eia.gov/pub/oil_gas/petroleum/analysis_publications/chronology/petroleumchronology2000.htm#T_13_, as of 07.05.2012, 21:45.
[66] An example would be the German 'Der Spiegel', who predicted the Iraqi invasion in a small article on 23.07.1990, describing Saddam as an increasingly mad man: Der Spiegel, 30/1990, http://www.spiegel.de/spiegel/print/d-13501855.html, as of 09.05.2012, 23:56.
[67] Iraq – Kuwait (1990-1991), Conflict Profile, Political Economy Research Institute, University Massachusetts Amherst, http://www.peri.umass.edu/fileadmin/pdf/Iraq3.pdf; as of 08.05.2012, 23:47.

the Iraqi leaders and a few close observers of Iraqi politics,[68] but also because the possible outcome was far from foreseeable. After all, even professional observers, like the Chinese high command, were later surprised by how easy it was for the coalition forces to break the Iraqi military resistance.[69] One must not forget that in 1990 the disastrous Vietnam War was just 15 years ago. Its unpleasant memories acted as a slide against which the chances for success in Iraq were measured.

Following our framework's indicators, it seems to be unnecessary to discuss whether the first Gulf Crisis can be classified as a rare event. After all, the 1991 war has been canonized as the first 'Gulf War' in the history books and in popular culture and certainly can be regarded as a unique historical event.[70] Finally, the global impact of the Gulf crisis cannot be overestimated, since on the long term it should again change the Middle Eastern balance of power and had a deep and long-lasting effect on businesses and the global economy as a whole. Thus, we can classify it as a 'Black Swan', even though the price jump, if measured in inflation adjusted terms, was not as dramatic as the one during the 1970s oil crisis. After all, almost overnight Iraqi daily crude oil output fell from about 3.5 million barrels per day to literally zero, due to the trade embargo imposed by UN resolution 661[71] - a situation that should be reversed only during the second half of the 1990s.[72] But why was the impact of production losses less severe than during the 1970s? First of all, in the meantime many countries had organized themselves in the IEA and built up substantial strategic oil reserves, parts of which were now released in order to ease the pressure on the markets. The US, for instance, had been a net importer prior to the crisis, but now began to export refined products to more challenged markets like Western Europe. Furthermore, businesses like the Aviation industry, for which the oil price is a vital issue, were able to gain protection against price volatility by accessing the new futures markets. Finally, the experiences of the previous

---

[68] It has to be remarked – in all fairness – that the signs for a dramatic action by the Iraqi regime were certainly there and the conflict between Iraq and Kuwait was far from being a secret. Furthermore, the war with Iran had weakened the country economically and it was desperate to ease the pressure. However, as discussed in the earlier chapters, just as so often we now see these signs ex post facto and thus out of a certain context, being biased by the knowledge of what actually happened. For a discussion of this matter please see: http://www.peri.umass.edu/fileadmin/pdf/Iraq3.pdf; as of 08.05.2012, 23:47.

[69] http://de.wikipedia.org/wiki/Zweiter_Golfkrieg#cite_note-2, as of 09.05. 2012, 21:32.

[70] A census which ignores the Iraqi-Iranian war from 1980 till 1988 and is, therefore, often criticized, however, nevertheless widely used.

[71] The full wording of the resolution can be found under: http://www.fas.org/news/un/iraq/sres/sres0661.htm, as of 09.05.2012, 23:25.

[72] Historic Iraqi crude output data compiled by WTRG Economics in 2011 can be found on WTRG's webpage: http://www.wtrg.com/oil_graphs/PAPRPIQ.gif, as of 09.05.2012, 22:39.

oil shocks had taught companies and consumers to build up redundancies by increasing efficiency and developing alternative energy usage abilities, which allowed for more flexibility.[73] Consumers could just switch from one resource to the other instead of just standing by and waiting for better times like in the 1970s.

Besides, from a consumer's perspective, better times were just about to arrive. The resolution of the Iraq crisis caused prices to fall quickly. They should stay at low levels throughout the 1990s. The fall of the Iron curtain opened a whole new world of resource exploration, since the technology used in the oil rich regions of the former Soviet Union was old and inefficient. Finally, countries like Azerbaijan, Kazakhstan or Russia, gained access to modern Western technologies and capital. At the same time, the industrial break down in many former Eastern Bloc countries decreased demand, while the supply from OPEC as well as from non-OPEC states was increasing. Hence, the 1990s saw historically low price levels, arriving at the lowest point when the Asian Financial crisis hit in 1997. Perhaps, the most important result of these developments was a change in the strategic focus of many energy firms. Confronted with low prices and high risks, they decided to increase their efficiency and organizational leverage by merging with competitors, forming giant multinational firms like ExxonMobil or BP Amoco. We shall later discuss, whether this was a positive development form a 'Black Swan' exposure point of view. However, for now, we will proceed with an event, that changed the international landscape again and had stark repercussions on people's lives, many of which can be felt still today.

3.1.6. 9/11 and its aftermath

We already discussed the events of 9/11 as a prototypical example of a 'Black Swan'. And indeed, it seems safe to say, that the terrorist attacks on the World Trade Centre in 2001 are certainly the key for the understanding of a big part of contemporary global history during the first decade of the 21st century. Although it would be redundant to discuss the event again in too much detail, in order to further substantiate the argument of this paper, a small analysis seems to be appropriate.

A handful of Islamist extremists changed the course of history by hijacking a couple of airplanes and using them as weapons of terror: 9/11 shocked the Western public and hit

---

[73]http://www.eia.gov/pub/oil_gas/petroleum/analysis_publications/chronology/petroleumchronology2000.htm#T_13_, as of 11.05.2012, 15:43.

government agencies completely off guard. Most importantly for this paper, not only did the chain of events of that day terrify surprised observers on a global level, but it also had the most severe effects on the energy business. After all, 9/11 proved to be not just a single extreme event, but it should trigger other high impact events like the wars in Afghanistan and Iraq. It encouraged the American government to stronger intervene in Arab affairs and it ultimately contributed also to the aggravation of existing conflicts, like the one in the Middle East. Thus, 9/11 was an absolutely surprising and sufficiently rare high impact event, or as Taleb put it:

"[...] had the risk been reasonably conceivable on September 10, it would not have happened. If such a possibility were deemed worthy of attention, fighter planes would have circled the sky above the twin towers, airplanes would have had locked bulletproof doors, and the attack would not have taken place, period."[74]

But what were the immediate consequences regarding energy? Certainly, among the effects were enormous insecurity and even fear in the markets as well as among consumers. After all, airlines were grounded and people in the Western world were afraid of further attacks. Recession lay in the air, famously documented by George Bush's appeal to Americans to go out and do some shopping.[75] Beginning with September 11, crude oil price levels began to rise to unforeseen heights, only stopping when with arrival of the global financial crisis in 2007/2008. From levels between 20-30 USD in 2001, prices should climb to more than 100 USD per Gallon of crude oil in 2007. Even prices way beyond that number were seriously discussed. Soon concerns were raised, that prices would never return to levels below 100 USD per Gallon. And yet, with the financial crisis, also this price bubble burst and levels returned to less than 60 USD per Gallon, only if however, to just rise again shortly later. The point is, that the events of 9/11 proved to be an enormously strong trigger for the subsequent price rally. Certainly, the accelerated rise of new Powers like China, Brazil and India caused an ever rising new demand and was responsible for a fair share of the pressure on

---

[74] http://www.nytimes.com/2007/04/22/books/chapters/0422-1st-tale.html?_r=2, as of 12.05.2012, 18:21.
[75] http://usgovinfo.about.com/od/thepresidentandcabinet/a/did-bush-say-go-shopping-after-911.htm, as of 12.05.2012, 19:57. However, it has to be remarked that apparently Bush never really made that statement. Rather, a journalist tried to condense the following interview answer: "I ask your continued participation and confidence in the American economy". Nevertheless, the fame the statement achieved, tells a lot about the mentality of the time.

the markets. However, politically the post-September 11 discourse overshadowed every-thing else on the international level. Although the wars in Afghanistan and Iraq were certainly high impact events, they were by no means 'Black Swans'. Rather they slowly developed out of the basic crisis situation and were directly linked to the complete change in the political landscape caused by the terrorist attacks. Instead of securing American influ-ence in the Islamic world or at least oil price stability, however, the wars brought even more instability and resulted in rising oil prices. Authoritarian regimes like the ones in Venezuela, Russia and Iran gained political influence thanks to their increased export revenues and in the Middle East the Islamist's popularity reached new peaks. Many accused the US-American government of having miscalculated their policies, leading to severe political repercussions and human suffering. But although many exponents of the Bush-Administration later claimed to have been surprised completely by the events[76], it is safe to say that only few critiques failed to warn of possible failure in advance.[77] Thus, by no means were the generic consequences of the invasions of 2001 and 2003 unforeseeable, but they created additional exposure to new dangers, or as Taleb, more generally remarks:

"[…] wars are fundamentally unpredictable (and we do not know it). Owing to this misunder-standing of the casual chains between policy and actions, we can easily trigger Black Swans thanks to aggressive ignorance-like a child playing with a chemistry kit."[78]

Despite that, the wars in Afghanistan and Iraq had long preludes and developed over a certain period of time. They did not hit suddenly by surprise and, therefore, lack some of the constituting criteria of a 'Black Swan'.

Consequently, they have to be regarded rather as effects and not as autonomous impacts themselves. As such, they just illustrate the enormous impact 9/11 had on the global political and economic system. It especially underlines Taleb's finding that the increasing interdependence of the globalized world actually increases the impact and, thus, the risks that come with 'Black Swan' hits. Just like in grid systems, one short circuit can eliminate the

---

[76] As for example Colin Powell: http://www.newsmax.com/Newsfront/AME-AMERICAME-ANNOTATED-ASIA/2012/05/03/id/437974, as of 12.05.2012, 23:18.
[77] As for example the then French President Jacques Chirac, who defended France's position in an interview: http://www.david-morrison.org.uk/other-documents/chirac-20030310.htm, as of 12.05.2012, 23:27.
[78] http://www.nytimes.com/2007/04/22/books/chapters/0422-1st-tale.html?pagewanted=2&_r=2, as of 12.05.2012, 18:21.

whole system. Since the crude oil price is heavily linked to global developments, its generation seems to be ever stronger exposed to 'Black Swan' events and their impact. After all,
the most striking feature of all the beforehand examined events is our "[...] inability to
predict outliers [, which] implies the inability to predict the course of history, given the share
of these events in the dynamics of events."[79] That basically means, that although we learned
from our analysis, that 'Black Swans' time and again completely changed the oil related
landscape, we did not learn anything about possible future events. By their very nature, they
are completely unpredictable and yet, their impact is most significant. Thus, all we can
conclude is that 'Black Swans' will happen and that they will render all our basic assumptions
obsolete.

By no means, however, does that mean that we should abandon all efforts and give way to
cheap fatalism. After all, even though there is no way to avoid 'Black Swans' completely,
given our increasingly complex world, still there are measures that help to mitigate their
impact. In order to learn more about these measures, we shall now proceed with analyzing
electricity and its relevance for our topic.

3.2. Electricity – a versatile necessity in times of crisis

3.2.1. The role of electricity prices

Since we established earlier, that the electricity price is not driven by a single international
market, but rather by a mixture of global factors and regional peculiarities, it makes sense to
limit the scope a little bit. Supposedly, mature economies with a strong need for electricity
should be the ones with the highest 'Black Swan' risk exposure, since any stark development
on the electricity market also hits the rest of the economy. However, any modern country or
region would suffer greatly from high electricity prices or blackouts. Therefore, instead of
examining a more or less homogenous global market, like in the case of crude oil, it is
necessary to focus on more specific local settings and cases. After all, for technical reasons,
electric grid systems are still a regional phenomenon, at best. Usually the access to electricity is organized on the regional or national level. Thus, there is no global unified market with
global prices, like in the case of oil. Rather, price levels strongly vary between different

---

[79] http://www.nytimes.com/2007/04/22/books/chapters/0422-1st-tale.html?pagewanted=2&_r=2, as of
12.05.2012, 18:21.

markets and so do infrastructure, regulation and competition, as we already explored earlier on in this paper. Furthermore, there are many different methods for producing electricity: From fossil fuel carburation or nuclear energy to alternatives like wind or solar. Consequently, each energy market also has a different energy mix, which comes with different kinds of risks in each case. All these factors make electricity a much more complex field of analysis. Rather than following a historic chain of events, like we did with crude oil, therefore, we must now focus on high impact events that were perhaps not so relevant on the global, but were quite important on a local level. Although they are, therefore, unrelated in terms of a historic narrative, they might yet be similar enough in order to allow for common conclusions. Above all, we have to decide on whether or not these events can be categorized as 'Black Swans' according to our paper's theoretical framework.

3.2.2. The California Energy Crisis

The California Energy crisis is largely seen today as a case study in failed deregulation. However, it is also an example of corporate fraudulent behavior and - less famously - of the impact unexpected weather conditions can have on the balance between supply and demand. But indeed, the catastrophic serious of events, that should lead to extraordinary price peaks and even blackouts, happened against the background of the energy market deregulation, put into legislation in 1996. The bill foresaw that the existing transmission network would be operated by an independent operator, while California Utilities should divest their production plants and purchase electricity from private producers at market prices at a newly created public exchange. The idea was to stir up competition and to increase efficiency. However, it turned out, that the private producers, in reality had no incentive to create more production capacity, which would have required huge further investments. Rather they were enabled to merely maintain their assets and wait for prices to rise. Because prices at the exchange were completely deregulated, Utilities had to pay increasingly absurd amounts in order to purchase electricity. On the other hand, due to caps on consumer prices, they were not able to transmit the price pressure coming from the supply side to the consumers. In consequence, demand did not sufficiently adapt to the increasing wholesale price levels, which drove some of the utilities into bankruptcy, forcing the Californian state to step in and bail them out.[80] But not only did the private producers not invest; they even willingly shut down plants in order to further increase the electricity price. In order to further drive up wholesale prices and, thereby, their excessive margins, some of the producers even applied fraudulent measures. For instance, there is plenty of proof that Enron in the midst of the crisis tried to manipulate prices by shutting down its plants, despite the fact that the state of California had declared to be in a state of energy emergency. Enron operated clandestinely and willingly broke federal law that requested all plants to produce at full capacity. On January 17th 2001, a major blackout hit California, just after Enron shut down another plant under the pretext to do some necessary maintenance work. Later investigations revealed, that Enron's management arbitrarily shut the plant down, encouraging the local staff to camouflage it as a maintenance job.[81]

But was the Californian electricity crisis the result of a 'Black Swan'? It seems, in retrospect, hard to believe, that beforehand none of the law-makers realized, that the 1996 law effectively created a price trap. Nevertheless, at the time the law was passed, there was literally no opposition:

"The complex bill passed with no dissenting votes, although later lawmakers admitted that many hadn't understood it. Gov. Pete Wilson signed it on Sept. 23, 1996." [82]

In fact, not only legislators but a vast majority of all the stakeholders agreed beforehand, that the deregulation would be beneficial for everyone: Consumers would benefit from lower prices, plants would be run more efficiently because of a less monopolistic supply structure and the utilities would get some payback on their long term asset investments by selling them to the new private operators.[83]

It appears, that the state representatives were blinded by wishful thinking, or rather, the somewhat ideological claim, that deregulation per se would be beneficial. It was not - and the reasons for the resulting market failure were manifold. While consumers had not much

---

[80] A timeline of the events can be found under:
http://www.pbs.org/wgbh/pages/frontline/shows/blackout/california/timeline.html, as of 14.07.2012, 12:03.
[81] Egan, Timothy: Tapes Show Enron Arranged Plant Shutdown, in: The New York Times, 04.02.2005,
http://www.nytimes.com/2005/02/04/national/04energy.html?_r=1&ex=1107666000&en=01449ebf62df572e
&ei=5070, as of 13.07.2012, 11:40.
[82] http://www.sfgate.com/news/article/THE-ENERGY-CRUNCH-A-YEAR-LATER-State-s-2834535.php, as of
13.07.2012, 15:51.
[83] Ibid.

incentive to save energy - let alone to change their suppliers - the utilities and the grid operator had to buy at almost every price from the private producers, in order to avoid blackouts. At the same time, the lack of investments into new production plants since the mid-1990s met with an increasing demand coming from the newly booming Californian economy. And on top of all that still came the fraudulent behavior of companies like Enron. The result was the exact opposite of what the deregulation plan had aimed for: Blackouts, excessive prices and even state bailout of the failing utilities, implying huge financial damages to the Californian economy and the tax payer. In the first year alone, retail prices tripled, while wholesale prices should eventually even reached levels of about 800% above the pre-deregulation prices.[84] All that happened within the timeframe of about two years and caused also a lot of political turmoil. Governor Gray Davis, who actually had been popular among voters, became the target of public discontent and had to hand over his office to 'Governator' Arnold Schwarzenegger, after being the only second Governor in US-American history, who had been recalled by the electorate before the planned end of his tenure. Davies was later said to have remarked about his personal failure: "It's a bummer to govern in bad times."[85]

But still, apologies aside, shouldn't actors have foreseen at least some of what happened? Energy consultant Susan L. Pope argues, that this was impossible, saying that:

"A more complete examination of the data challenges these conclusions, providing a picture more like that of a perfect storm, in which a number of unfavorable demand/supply events improbably coincided, leading to increases in electricity prices that are understandable in hindsight."[86]

Critics might disagree with that, but they also have to concede, that even if some of the events like the price rises, could have been foreseen, knowledge about them had been distributed unequally, favoring some of the private producer companies like Enron, who used their knowledge in order to further manipulate the market in their favor. Thus, for consumers and politicians like Gray Davis, the events indeed came as a surprise. Neverthe-

---

[84] Data has been taken from the chart of table 3 in the Appendix.
[85] Yergin: The Quest, p. 393.
[86] Pope, Susan L.: California Electricity Price Spikes: An Update on the Facts, http://www.hks.harvard.edu/hepg/Papers/Pope_CA.price.spike.update_12-9-02.pdf, as of 14.07.2012, 19:07. It has to be mentioned; however, that Pope's paper was partly financed by an energy merchant firm, with generating assets also in California and, thus, some critics might not share her views.

less, he and his government were later held responsible for the crisis. Many observers concluded that the apparent market failure was mainly caused by a lack of sufficient regulation, despite having good monitoring in place.[87] Others, like James L. Sweeny even argue that the crisis was caused by a complete failure of the political leadership that, first, chose to leave everything to the market and when faced with the challenge of the supply crisis, suddenly overreacted, making the damage even worse.[88] Or in other words: The political leadership of California was completely surprised, had made no plans for any such situation and consequently was reduced to just reacting on the deteriorating chain of events. In conclusion, it seems, that the events leading to the crisis could not have been reasonably foreseen by the main actors involved, although there is certainly no lack of ex post facto explanations, that claim that the government should have been prepared better or should have applied a completely different reform altogether. But even if we would assume, that the government indeed would have made foreseeable regulatory mistakes, there are many other factors that it cannot be blamed for. For instance, just in coincidence with the deregulation, California was hit by unusually dry weather, reducing its hydropower generation capacities by at least 20%. On top of that, 2001 brought an extremely cold winter, increasing the electricity demand for California by 5.8% versus the expected rates. [89] Therefore, Van Drosten and Taylor concluded already back then, that "[...] the reductions in supply and increases in demand that resulted in wholesale electricity price increases are the result of natural weather variation interacting with market forces. No state politician, regulator, or businessman could have headed them off.".[90] In consequence, also considering the volatile price levels, that went from below 50 USD per MWh in April 2000 to more than 400 USD per MWh at around year end and back to below 50 USD per MWh in autumn 2001[91]; furthermore, also considering the severe blackouts, it is justified to call the California Electricity Crisis a rare and ex ante unpredictable, extreme impact event. Hence, here we go with another 'Black Swan'.

---

[87] For example: Wolak, Frank A.: Lessons from the California Electricity Crisis, in: Griffin, James M.: Electricity deregulation: choices and challenges, The University of Chicago Press, Chicago, 2005, page 179-181.

[88] Sweeney, James L.: The California Electricity Crisis, Hoover Institution Press Publication, Stanford, 2002, page 2.

[89] Taylor, Jerry/ Van Doren, Peter: California's Electricity Crisis: What's Going On, Who's to Blame, and What to Do, Policy Analysis no. 406, July 2001, page 7.

[90] Taylor, Jerry/ Van Doren, Peter: California's Electricity Crisis: What's Going On, Who's to Blame, and What to Do, Policy Analysis no. 406, July 2001, page 8.

[91] Weare, Christopher: The California Electricity Crisis: Causes and Policy Options, Public Policy Institute of California, San Francisco, 2003, p. 1 and following.

Just like in the crude oil related cases we discussed earlier, also for the California Electricity Crisis, the extraordinarily high price were a constituting element as well as a 'Black Swan' - indicator. Perhaps even more important, though, were the rolling blackouts that marked the total breakdown of the system. It actually seems that in the field of electricity, blackouts could be an even more important indicator than price levels, since no electricity is even worse than too expensive one. We shall further examine this idea with the next case, in which also weather played an important role.

3.2.3. The 2008 Central Asia Energy crisis

In winter 2008, Central Asia experienced abnormally cold temperatures, which went below -20 degree Celsius and caused avalanches, traffic breakdowns and snow storms, cutting people of from outside supplies. Despite gas and oil shortages, the worst problem was an unexpected, acute lack of electricity, which especially hit the already rather poor population of Tajikistan. But not only did temperatures fall below record lows, also the water levels decreased significantly. This had a devastating effect, since Tajikistan till this day heavily depends on its hydro power plants, which were now suddenly unable to deliver. Further-more, since also Tajikistan's neighbors Uzbekistan and Kazakhstan suffered from gas short-ages and cold, they could not assist the former Soviet Republic with additional electricity supplies, as they traditionally had done in the past. Rather, this time they even decreased their badly needed gas deliveries. Consequently, the Tajik economy and - above all - ordinary people and their families suffered greatly. Traffic broke down, homes remained without heating and lights and many people were even cut-off from food supplies. Even in the capital Dushanbe, only crucial facilities like hospitals, key industry plants and government offices received unlimited electric energy, whereas normal homes had to fall back to 'traditional' methods of heating and cooking. The authorities were not able anymore to guarantee for basic supplies, let alone rescue services. At the same time, the government raised electricity prices by 20%, allegedly in order to be able to repay its World Bank debts. Finally, Tajikistan asked for international assistance, facing famines and a possible total blackout. Subsequent-ly, the UNOCHA distributed 5.2 million USD in emergency response money, to mitigate civilian suffering.[92]

---

[92]The paragraph above is based on information from:
http://www.eurasianet.org/departments/insight/articles/pp011308.shtml, as of 10.07.2012, 21:33; Antelava,

What is most striking about this case, is, that it was not the soaring prices, but the constant menace of power outages, that posed the biggest threat. It therefore makes no sense to try to quantify the crisis' impact via the electricity price levels. Of course, its impact on the economy and, above all, the population of Tajikistan were most severe. However, by no means did price levels rise as extremely as in the case of the California Electricity Crisis. More importantly, the almost complete blackout marked a far-reaching economic and humanitarian breakdown, the global impact of which was only limited by the relatively low economic maturity of the Central Asian economy. It seems, therefore, save to say, that the crisis was definitely an extreme impact event. Furthermore, temperature levels as cold as in 2008, hadn't been measured in the region for more than fifty years up until that point. That, in combination with the unusually low water levels, which caused the loss of the important hydro power, could hardly have been foreseen. Thus, the events that caused the crisis were also sufficiently rare and certainly hit the country and the international community by surprise. Consequently, the 2008 Central Asian Energy crisis clearly qualifies as a 'Black Swan'. As expected, due to the localized structure of electric energy supply, it hit regionally, rather than internationally. However, a similar scenario in regions more vital for the global economic network, could have been much more devastating, in terms of financial impact. Exactly such an event will be examined with the next case.

3.2.4. The 2011 Tsunami

The combined disasters caused by the Tohoku earthquake in 2011 were one of the worst catastrophes in Japanese history. With more than 15,000 death and even more injured, the human suffering was enormous. As is widely known, the earthquake, being the strongest ever measured in Japan up until this point, caused a Tsunami, which subsequently resulted in a nuclear meltdown in three reactors of the Fukushima-Daiichi nuclear power plant. If the event wasn't so tragic, its setup would sound outright absurd, even if it was a Hollywood movie plot. And yet everything happened in reality, bringing us right back to our topic, which is rare and unpredictable extreme impact events. After all, in many respects, the Japanese Tsunami catastrophe prototypically fulfilled all the conditions of a 'Black Swan', hitting the

---

Natalia: Tajikistan 'facing food crisis', in: http://news.bbc.co.uk/2/hi/asia-pacific/7231528.stm, as of 10.07.2012, 21:43; and Situation Report No. 4 – Tajikistan – Cold Wave/Compound crisis (25 February 2008), UNOHCA.

entire globe by surprise. However, for the sake of our argument, we shall focus just on those aspects that were closely related to electricity.

The greater region of Tokyo is one of the biggest electricity hubs of the world. TEPCO, the owner company of the Fukushima power plant, alone, produces about as much energy as all of Italy. An in-depth review study of the IEA revealed in 2008, that the Kanto region, including Tokyo, had a production capacity of about 78 GW on average. Immediately after the disaster hit, nuclear capacity of about 9.7 GW and fossil fuel capacity of 9.5 GW were lost, either due to physical damage or controlled emergency shut-downs. According to the 2008 capacity data, this would mean a sudden loss of about one quarter of total capacity – a major blow for one of the technologically most advanced and energy depended regions of the world. Unsurprisingly, a series of rolling blackouts was the immediate consequence.[93] The situation was further aggravated by the fact, that for historic reasons the Japanese grid system is divided into two parts with almost no possibility of interchange.[94] Therefore, it was not possible to transfer much needed backup energy from the rather un-impacted southeastern part of the country to the affected area. Surprisingly though, despite widely spread fears, there were no major cases of electricity shortages during the following summer. This is all the more surprising, given the fact that already in May nuclear power generation was down to 51% of nominal capacity, reaching only 36% after July. Although the central government, out of fear of blackouts, did not request any immediate shut-downs, one plant after the other went offline, due to scheduled maintenance. Subsequently, the responsible local authorities denied the restarts, effectively slowly eliminating nuclear power from the Japanese energy mix.[95] All this was only made possible, however, because most Japanese followed the requests of the government to safe energy wherever possible. Offices switched off air-condition, the famous Tokyo advertisement lights went black and people limited their private consumption to a minimum. Even so, the Japanese industry, which was already hit

---

[93]The data cited in this paragraph was taken from: IMPACT OF EARTHQUAKES AND TSUNAMIS ON ENERGY SECTORS IN JAPAN (IEA 15 March 2011), IEA/OECD, 2011, http://www.iea.org/files/japanfactsheet.pdf, as of 16.07.2012, 22:55.

[94] Eastern Japan started its grid system with an AEG generator, running with 50 Hz, while Western Japan began with a 60 Hz General Electric generator. For further details: Williams, Martyn: A legacy from the 1800s leaves Tokyo facing blackouts, http://www.itworld.com/business/140626/legacy-1800s-leaves-tokyo-facing-blackouts, as of 17.07.2012, 21:34.

[95] Data taken from: Cooke, Stephanie: After Fukushima, Does Nuclear Power Have a Future?, http://www.nytimes.com/2011/10/11/business/energy-environment/after-fukushima-does-nuclear-power-have-a-future.html?pagewanted=2&_r=1, as of 17.07.2012, 22:08.

hard by the Earthquake and the Tsunami, suffered from the electricity shortage. Car manu-facturing plants, depending on a just-in-time production schedule, faced long delays and in many high tech industries even global supply chains were disrupted.[96] Also internationally the Japanese disaster had serious consequences for electricity generation: In Germany, the government, up until that point had been in favor of nuclear energy. Now, it suddenly decided to abandon it for good. In Israel, Venezuela and Taiwan plans to construct new nuclear power plants were scrapped. Many other countries and even China, with its enor-mous thirst for energy, decided to thoroughly review their existing plans.[97] Some observers even claim, that nuclear energy's reputation has been tarnished forever. Indeed, in many countries, including Japan, public opinion is not anymore in favor of maintaining it. But still, many experts and plant operators claim that nuclear energy is generally safe and the growing global need for energy makes the nuclear option a necessary addition to the energy mix for a significant number of countries.

In fact, it is therefore not entirely misplaced, to ask whether the Fukushima accident, with its grave consequences, could not have been avoided. After all, although the Earthquake and the Tsunami per se were of course unpredictable natural events, it was generally known, that natural disasters happen frequently in the region. The fact, that one of the biggest nuclear power plants in the world had been constructed just next to the coastline - danger-ously exposed to the forces of nature - seems to be outrageous in retrospect. Consequently, the focus of public attention slowly switched from the natural disaster towards human error. A CNN report sums up the argument, saying that:

"The epic disaster at Fukushima Daiichi represents failure at almost every level, from how the Japanese government regulates nuclear power, to how TEPCO managed critical details of the crisis under desperate circumstances."[98]

Thus, was the disaster at least partly foreseeable, after all? Perhaps, but more likely this is ex-post-facto thinking. Although there are reports about discussions about the possible

---

[96] A more detailed analysis of that issue and the therefrom deriving problems can be found in an article published in The Economist in March 2011: http://www.economist.com/node/18486015, as of 18.08.2012, 00:50.
[97] Cooke, Stephanie: After Fukushima, Does Nuclear Power Have a Future?, http://www.nytimes.com/2011/10/11/business/energy-environment/after-fukushima-does-nuclear-power-have-a-future.html?pagewanted=2&_r=1, as of 17.07.2012, 22:08.

[98] http://tech.fortune.cnn.com/2012/04/20/fukushima-daiichi/, as of 17.07.2012, 23:58.

impacts of a Tsunami on the power plant before the incident, there are many indicators that show that everyone involved simply out-ruled the possibility of an accident of that scale beforehand. For instance, there was an emergency outpost about five kilometers away from the plant, which was supposed to serve as an ad hoc command center in case of an accident. When the accident actually happened, it turned out, that the command outpost was not even isolated against nuclear radiation, rendering it completely useless towards its original purpose.[99] Consequently, a commission charged by the Japanese government with the task to investigate the incident, concluded, that although the nuclear accident in theory might have been avoided, it seems that in praxis neither TEPCO nor the authorities were sufficiently prepared for a natural disaster of that scale. Rather, both were blinded by a 'myth of security', which deemed the possibility of an accident so unlikely, that nobody seriously bothered to prepare for it.[100] As in the case of 9/11, all the pieces of the puzzle were available beforehand, however, they only fit perfectly together in retrospect.

Now, if 'Black Swans' are really unpredictable and, thus, unavoidable, what lessons can we possibly learn from all the cases we reviewed in this paper? The answer is: Nothing that will enable us to stop 'Black Swans' from happening, but still a lot. In the next chapter well shall now see, what that means.

---

[99] Ibid.

[100] The commission's findings were first reported via the international press, as for example in: Ein fataler „Sicherheitsmythos", faz.net, http://www.faz.net/aktuell/politik/ausland/japan-ein-fataler-sicherheitsmythos-11829335.html, as of 23.07.2012, 16:32.

4. Is protection possible? Discussion and outline of risk mitigation measures

Time and again the landscape of energy has been reshaped by unprecedented, rare extreme impact events. The 'Black Swan' disproved all predictive models and rebutted the forecasts. And most likely, it will keep doing so in the future. That is perhaps the first important lesson we can learn from the cases we reviewed. It implies, that it is rather unlikely, that our predictions about the near, or even the far future are of much practical value, especially if they are fairly concrete, like in the case of price forecasts. Nevertheless, there are ways to gain some protection in terms of mitigating a 'Black Swan's' impact. First, we shall now review what Taleb has to tell us about that and then we shall apply this knowledge on what we have learned about the world of energy during our analysis.

As the cases above showed, there is no such thing as perfect protection. Nevertheless, according to Taleb, there are some principles that can help to improve robustness. They do not provide perfect protection from 'Black Swans', but may help to mitigate its impact, when applied.

First of all, any actor in the field has to make sure he truly understands the limits of his knowledge. Otherwise he might apply a wrong cure to a complex situation that might have worked out much better without any interference in the first place. After all, sometimes doing nothing is better than doing anything just to do something.

Furthermore, as already discussed more generally in chapter 2, redundancy is a good tool in order to mitigate 'Black Swan' impact. Its effectiveness has been proven in many practical fields, like for instance the Aviation industry or in medicine. Redundancy basically provides insurance against all-out failure, although it unfortunately reduces efficiency. And there is still another angle to it. As much as redundancy is desirable, over-optimization is not: Being in a specialized but lucrative niche might provide the niche-holder with huge temporary windfalls, but it will prove to be fatal, once it disappears, leaving the specialist with a lack of alternatives.

Yet another important factor is size. According to Taleb it is preferable to have a system comprised of a couple of smaller, more agile entities than one 'to-big-to-fail'-kind of structure. There are many examples for that, one of which comes from IT, where the danger to lose one's data in case of an incident, is much bigger with a mainframe-based system than with a network of many small servers all around the globe. The example again underlines the important point, that there is no complete protection, just impact mitigation: Whereas in the case of the unexpected loss of a main frame computer all data saved on it is lost instantly, in a network based system, losing one or more of the servers means the loss of only some data. Thus, a data loss per se cannot be avoided. However, its severity can be considerably limited. Once the US-Military grasped that point, they developed what we know as the Internet today, which, some scientists believe, thanks to its decentralized structure could even survive a nuclear war.[101]

Finally, Taleb warns, to not mistake a lack of volatility for an absence of risk. Rather, he claims, the absence of volatility is a strong indicator for high 'Black Swan' exposure. In order to understand the notion behind that idea, it is helpful to consider what Taleb added to this thought at a discussion panel in Frankfurt am Main in May 2012: He elaborated further on some thoughts about how to deal with 'Black Swans' preventively.[102] Reiterating that increasing size makes systems more fragile, especially if they systematically seek to erase deviations, he argued that instead of trying to prevent recurring small errors, systems should allow for them. This would help them to 'immunize' themselves against big, but rare errors that might otherwise kill a system that had been running perfectly up until that point. Using the example of small controlled fires, which are used in order to protect forests from conflagration, Taleb argues, that similar techniques could protect complex systems, like for instance the financial markets, from large scale failure by constantly attacking weak spots before they can develop into bigger problems. On the other hand, he finds, some systems are simply more fragile than others: They may prove resilient against thousands or even millions of small shocks, only to finally break, as soon as an outlier hits. To put the matter in a nutshell, according to Taleb's argument, error should be the rule and not the exception. Only if kept under constant stress, complex systems are able to spot and eliminate weaknesses and to raise awareness for the always looming possibility of failure. Furthermore,

---

[101] Although it is somewhat unclear, whether that was really the reason for creating the internet, the idea certainly played a role in its history. More details can be found under:
http://en.wikipedia.org/wiki/ARPANET#cite_note-5, as of 16.07.2012, 15:59.
[102] An abstract of these thoughts can be found in an article published in the German Frankfurter Allgemeine Zeitung: http://www.faz.net/aktuell/finanzen/fonds-mehr/bestseller-autor-nassim-taleb-aus-kleinen-fehlern-lernen-11745973.html, as of 10.05.2012, 23:27.

Taleb elaborates that the trail left by a row of recurring small errors, enables us to actually measure the fragility of systems. While 'Black Swans' are principally unpredictable, measuring a system's fragility at least can show us the severity of the 'Black Swan' exposure of a given system. In order to illustrate his point, Taleb provided the following example: In the global economic environment, financial systems based on debt are more fragile than systems based on stock markets, while among debt systems a privately financed one without state guarantees is less fragile than a publicly financed one, with full state liability. Following that thought, there seems to be an intrinsic trade-off: Achieving better protection from frequent small risks by increasing size also increases the exposure to large but rare risks. While for a big bank for instance, single small credit risks become insignificant, an all-out system failure - forcing a great number of small debtors to default simultaneously - hits with much more power.

Applying this insight to the energy business: Having constantly growing bigger enterprises, decreases the risk of bankruptcy due to single project's failure, however, raises the stakes in terms of systemic risks: Perfectly controlled, large organizations lose the ability to react flexibly on sudden changes. Enormous capital amounts become tied up in organizations that could prove worthless dinosaurs from one day to another, just like for instance, in case of an unexpected technological breakthrough or a high level liability accident. Within the last two decades, a lot of consolidation among producer companies has taken place. Smaller companies merged with others in order to gain efficiency through economies of scale. In the crude oil extraction business, exploration projects became more and more costly, partly because of the increased share of unconventional reserves. Generally, the accelerated globalization and the increased international economic interdependence favored the development of a few big multinational firms. In fact, among the 50 biggest companies of the world today, 13 are in the energy business, four of which are in the list's top ten and the biggest company of the world being the oil and gas giant ExxonMobil.[103] Certainly, this trend will continue, as new energy giants from emerging markets like China and Brazil will appear on the scene. This is dangerous, however, because each of these firms is now of a size and importance, that many would deem to be 'too big to fail'. Thus, the systemic impact of 'Black Swans' is potentially

---

[103] According to Forbes Magazine's list of the 2000 biggest companies of the world:
http://www.forbes.com/global2000/#p_1_s_a0_All%20industries_All%20countries_All%20states, as of 20.07.2012, 11:38.

enormous. The structure provides incentive to mitigate predictable risks and volatility by increasing size and efficiency. On the other hand this increases the potential impact severity of unsystematic risks and reduces redundancy. Consequently, it becomes more and more probable that a 'Black Swan' will hit the system and have a devastating impact.

But what can be done about that? After all, the obvious alternative that comes to mind – splitting up the existing big firms and establish stronger competition with a certain level of endemic failure – is quite counterintuitive and will meet strong resistance. Perhaps, the immediate answer lies rather in the field of redundancy improvement. As became clear throughout the different cases we examined, the crude oil based energy business is fairly globalized, with common international price levels. Shocks to the system are transmitted to every single part of the chain almost instantly via the crude oil world market price, making 'Black Swans' an imminent threat for the oil dependent world. The electricity based energy business on the other hand, is regionalized and more differentiated in terms of generation and transmission. Most likely, 'Black Swans' will hit the system on a local rather than on a global level. Therefore, their impact will be significantly smaller. In addition to that, it can be further reduced by inducing more redundancy. As we saw in the case of the 2011 Japanese earthquake and Tsunami, Japan and Germany were able to sustain electricity supply, even though they shut down most of their nuclear energy generation capacity, while Tajikistan with its very strong dependency on one single source of electricity faced severe blackouts.

In theory, electricity, which is less sensitive regarding 'Black Swan' impact, could take over big parts of the role, crude oil plays today for the global economy, provided that markets and governments will succeed in diversifying their generation portfolios and technology provides answers regarding the existing issues with storage and transmission. From transportation over production to yet other purposes, it could prove to be advantageous to reduce oil dependency by increasing the use of electric energy instead. First of all, thanks to the diverse electricity generation methods, this would increase redundancy, without even significantly decreasing energy supply efficiency. Perhaps even more importantly, it would also allow for smaller size firms in a healthy and competition driven market environment. Unlike in the past, today there are generation technologies, which can be utilized also with smaller investments. This would further open up the market to new entrants and lead to more decentralization and diversification regarding electricity generation. Still, at this point, this discourse is of course highly speculative, since many alternative technologies are not yet competitive in terms of production costs. Even so, electricity generation allows for a wide range of choices, whereas the oil supply depends on a complex production and distribution network in the hands of a few governments and corporate global players.

But even within the oil business, within certain limits Taleb's principles can be applied: Actors operating in the market should try to create redundancies, avoiding focusing too much on one specialized sector of the business - even if it seems to be the most profitable one at the moment. They should make sure to maintain a wide ranging portfolio of different assets and projects, none of which should become too important to fail. Finally, they should be very careful using strategic assumptions based on price predictions. As discussed in chapter 3, prices proved to be very sensitive regarding 'Black Swans' in the past and are, therefore, a weak foundation for any strategy. After all, the oil business by its very nature remains a capital and time intensive endeavor. Certainly there are structural pressures that favor large size. Marginal thinking dictates efficiency wherever possible. However, sooner or later the 'Black Swan' will hit and when it does, it will be the small and the fat and not the outsized and the starving who will survive. So if one cannot be small, one should better be fat. And if one cannot be fat one must be small and agile.

5. Summary and Conclusion

In this paper we examined the effect and significance of rare and unexpected extreme impact events on the energy related socio-economic system. Following the thoughts of Nassim Nicholas Taleb we called these events 'Black Swans' and characterized them as an intellectual proxy for unsystematic risks. These risks are usually neglected by analysts, because they are hardly quantifiable and often counter-intuitive. And yet they have a game-changing effect. By their very nature they are unavoidable. In consequence, we concluded that 'Black Swans' render the experience-based predictive models used in the energy business today, vastly useless and deprive market actors of the possibility to make detailed strategic plans for the future. Hoping to find ways to at least mitigate the impact of 'Black Swans', we embarked into the analysis of historic examples, using pre-defined criteria in order to identify 'Black Swans' and to quantify their impact.

Examining the historic impact of 'Black Swans', we observed that they played a vital role in the development of the modern energy landscape. Whenever they hit, they had an immediate impact on the balance between supply and demand. Therefore, we inferred, 'Black Swans' can be identified by sudden prices changes, providing us with a simple and robust indicator. This turned out to be especially true for the oil market. Because of global trade patterns and the unified crude oil world market price, 'Black Swans' that affected the oil related socio-economic system usually had a global impact, mainly reflected in price shocks. Examples for that were the oil crisis in the 1970s, the Iran crisis and the Gulf war at the beginning of the 1990s. 'Black Swans' that mainly affected the electricity systems, on the other hand, had typically a rather local impact, sometimes reflected by price volatility but always resulting in blackouts. This was observed, for instance, in consequence of the California energy crisis one decade ago, or during the Central Asia Energy crisis in 2008.

Thus, there is an important difference between oil and electricity regarding 'Black Swan' impact, which derives from the structural characteristics of both systems. While the oil supply system is organized in an international network structure with big global actors, electricity is usually generated and used locally by regional producers and consumers. Furthermore, unlike the oil business, which is based on crude oil alone, electricity producers can utilize a wide range of different resources and generation techniques. This makes them more flexible and reduces 'Black Swan' exposure.

Reviewing Taleb's recommendations regarding 'Black Swan' protection, we concluded, that it is unfortunately impossible to avoid 'Black Swan' hits altogether, however, their impact can be mitigated by a couple of structural adjustments. Most importantly, any exposed system or entity should try to increase redundancy. On a more systemic level, regulators or managers should try to diminish single unit size but increase the overall unit number, while enabling potent mechanisms - like for instance well-functioning free markets - that allow for constant small error checks - controlled forest fires so to say. When applied properly, these measures can considerably diminish 'Black Swan' impact on a single entity and on a systemic level as well.

Since these technics comply with the natural structure of the electricity business, we concluded that it would be beneficial to replace crude oil derivatives with electric energy wherever possible, because of the latter's lower 'Black Swan' exposure. A precondition for that is of course, that electricity producers diversify their production portfolios. Furthermore, regulators should assist the process by supporting a well regulated market environment that inhibits 'too big to fail'-kind of entities and allows for a healthy amount of competition - recurring small failures included. Finally, governments should aim for strategic redundancies, broadening their countries' generation and transmission portfolios without favoring any single source of energy in particular. To be sure, the biggest temptations for any involved actor - especially in business - are efficiency, optimization and growth. They intuitively make sense and do show results on the short term. After all, shareholders like to see their profits soar and governments love to shine in the bright light of their big national champions. But on the long run such a single-minded focus is dangerous, because it increases 'Black Swan' exposure. Since energy is the lifeblood of our economies, a safe and manifold secured supply is crucial. However, unmitigated 'Black Swans' are an imminent threat to that safety and stability. Therefore, effectiveness must take precedence over ostensive efficiency in order to safeguard people, businesses and whole countries' livelihoods. Alas, the 'Black Swan' cannot be tamed, but we can overcome some of its horror.

6. Bibliography

Books and Monographs:

Campanini, Massimo: Storia del Medio Oriente 1798 – 2006, Il Mulino, Bologna 2007.

Dallek, Robert: Nixon and Kissinger: Partner in Power, HarperCollins, New York, 2007.

Nasar, Sylvia: Grand Pursuit – The Story of Economic Genius, Simon&Schuster, New York, 2011.

Sorkin, Andrew Ross: Too Big To Fail, Penguin Books, New York, 2009.

Stöver, Bernd: Der Kalte Krieg 1947 – 1990: Geschichte eines radikalen Zeitalters, Beck, 2007.

Taleb, Nassim Nicholas: Fooled by Randomness – The Hidden Role of Chance in Life and in the Markets, Penguin Books, New York, 2007.

Taleb, Nassim Nicholas: The Black Swan: The Impact of the Highly Improbable, Penguin Books, New York, 2008.

Yergin, Daniel: The Prize – The Epic Quest for Oil, Money & Power, The Free Press, New York, 1991.

Yergin, Daniel: The Quest – Energy, Security, and the Remaking of the Modern World, Allen Lane, London, 2011.

Articles from Journals (including scientific articles or reports provided online):

BP Energy Outlook 2030, London, January 2012, http://www.bp.com/liveassets/bp_internet/globalbp/STAGING/global_assets/downloads/O/2012_2030_energy_outlook_booklet.pdf, as of 31.03.2012, 14:59.

Dermot Gately, "The Prospects for OPEC Five Years after 1973-74," European Economic Review, vol. 12 (October 1979), p. 378.

IMPACT OF EARTHQUAKES AND TSUNAMIS ON ENERGY SECTORS IN JAPAN (IEA 15 March 2011), IEA/OECD, 2011, http://www.iea.org/files/japanfactsheet.pdf, as of 16.07.2012, 22:55.

Iraq – Kuwait (1990-1991), Conflict Profile, Political Economy Research Institute, University Massachusetts Amherst, http://www.peri.umass.edu/fileadmin/pdf/Iraq3.pdf; as of 08.05.2012, 23:47.

Malcolm Brinded: Global Energy Outlook and Policy Implications, http://www-static.shell.com/static/media/downloads/speeches/brinded_london_28062011a.pdf, as of 31.03.2012, 14:24.

Pope, Susan L.: California Electricity Price Spikes: An Update on the Facts, http://www.hks.harvard.edu/hepg/Papers/Pope_CA.price.spike.update_12-9-02.pdf, as of 14.07.2012, 19:07.

Richard Nixon: "Address to the Nation About National Energy Policy.", November 25, 1973. Online by Gerhard Peters and John T. Woolley, The American Presidency Project. http://www.presidency.ucsb.edu/ws/index.php?pid=4051#axzz1rfyvqWkz, as of 10.04.2012, 23:52.

Situation Report No. 4 – Tajikistan – Cold Wave/Compound crisis (25 February 2008), UNOHCA, 2012.

Sweeney, James L.: The California Electricity Crisis, Hoover Institution Press Publication, Stanford, 2002, page 2.

Talib, Nassim Nicholas: The Black Swan: The Impact of the highly Improbable, The New York Times, 22.04.2007, http://www.nytimes.com/2007/04/22/books/chapters/0422-1st-tale.html?ex=1178769600&en=bdae1078f2b4a98c&ei=5070, as of 10.04.2012, 22:35.

Taylor, Jerry/ Van Doren, Peter: California's Electricity Crisis: What's Going On, Who's to Blame, and What to Do, Policy Analysis no. 406, July 2001, page 7.

The Outlook for Energy: A View to 2040, http://www.exxonmobil.com/Corporate/Files/news_pub_eo2012.pdf, as of 31.03.2012, 13:23.

Weare, Christopher: The California Electricity Crisis: Causes and Policy Options, Public Policy Institute of California, San Francisco, 2003.

Wolak, Frank A.: Lessons from the California Electricity Crisis, in: Griffin, James M.: Electricity deregulation: choices and challenges, The University of Chicago Press, Chicago, 2005, page 179-181.

WORLD ENERGY OUTLOOK 2011 FACTSHEET, IEA, http://www.worldenergyoutlook.org/docs/weo2011/factsheets.pdf, 23.03.2012, 23:47, page 1.

Website articles and other online resources:

Antelava, Natalia: Tajikistan 'facing food crisis', in: http://news.bbc.co.uk/2/hi/asia-pacific/7231528.stm, as of 10.07.2012, 21:43

Cooke, Stephanie: After Fukushima, Does Nuclear Power Have a Future?, http://www.nytimes.com/2011/10/11/business/energy-environment/after-fukushima-does-nuclear-power-have-a-future.html?pagewanted=2&_r=1, as of 17.07.2012, 22:08.

DoD News Briefing - Secretary Rumsfeld and Gen. Myers, 12.02.2002, http://www.defense.gov/transcripts/transcript.aspx?transcriptid=2636, as of 29.07.2012, 02:31.

Egan, Timothy: Tapes Show Enron Arranged Plant Shutdown, in: The New York Times, 04.02.2005, http://www.nytimes.com/2005/02/04/national/04energy.html?_r=1&ex=1107666000&en=01449ebf62df572e&ei=5070, as of 13.07.2012, 11:40.

http://de.wikipedia.org/wiki/Zweiter_Golfkrieg#cite_note-2, as of 09.05. 2012, 21:32.

http://en.wikipedia.org/wiki/ARPANET#cite_note-5, as of 16.07.2012, 15:59.

http://news.bbc.co.uk/2/hi/middle_east/2754103.stm, as of 06.05.2012, 11:31.

http://news.bbc.co.uk/2/hi/middle_east/3333995.stm, as of 07.04.2012, 18:42.

http://news.bbc.co.uk/onthisday/hi/dates/stories/september/30/newsid_3115000/3115476.stm, as of 13.03.2012, 13:12.

http://tech.fortune.cnn.com/2012/04/20/fukushima-daiichi/, as of 17.07.2012, 23:58.

http://usgovinfo.about.com/od/thepresidentandcabinet/a/did-bush-say-go-shopping-after-911.htm, as of 12.05.2012, 19:57.

http://www.bbc.co.uk/iplayer/episode/p00pfhq5/Business_Daily_Back_to_the_future/, as of 23.03.2012, 15:33.

http://www.brookings.edu/~/media/Files/Programs/ES/BPEA/1986_2_bpea_papers/1986b_bpea_gately_adelman_griffin.pdf, as of 30.04.2012, 18:48, page 242.

http://www.david-morrison.org.uk/other-documents/chirac-20030310.htm, as of 12.05.2012, 23:27.

http://www.economist.com/node/18486015, as of 18.08.2012, 00:50.

http://www.economist.com/node/21540275, The Economist, Nov 26th 2011, as of 03.05.2012, 12:32.

http://www.eia.gov/emeu/international/elecprih.html, as of 01.04.2012, 21:31

http://www.eia.gov/pub/oil_gas/petroleum/analysis_publications/chronology/petroleumchronology2000.htm#T_4_, as of 11.04.2012, 23:04.

http://www.eia.gov/pub/oil_gas/petroleum/analysis_publications/chronology/petroleumchronology2000.htm#T_4_, as of 11.04.2012, 23:04.

http://www.eia.gov/pub/oil_gas/petroleum/analysis_publications/chronology/petroleumchronology2000.htm#T_4_, as of 11.04.2012, 23:04.

http://www.eia.gov/pub/oil_gas/petroleum/analysis_publications/chronology/petroleumchronology2000.htm#T_4_, as of 11.04.2012, 23:04.

http://www.eia.gov/pub/oil_gas/petroleum/analysis_publications/chronology/petroleumchronology2000.htm#T_8_ as of 12.04.2012, 00:06.

http://www.eia.gov/pub/oil_gas/petroleum/analysis_publications/chronology/petroleumchronology2000.htm#T_10_, as of 30.04.2012, 18:24.

http://www.eia.gov/pub/oil_gas/petroleum/analysis_publications/chronology/petroleumch
ronology2000.htm#T_13_, as of 01.05.2012.

http://www.eia.gov/pub/oil_gas/petroleum/analysis_publications/chronology/petroleumch
ronology2000.htm#T_13_, as of 07.05.2012, 21:45.

http://www.eia.gov/pub/oil_gas/petroleum/analysis_publications/chronology/petroleumch
ronology2000.htm#T_13_, as of 11.05.2012, 15:43.

http://www.eurasianet.org/departments/insight/articles/pp011308.shtml, as of 10.07.2012,
21:33

http://www.fas.org/news/un/iraq/sres/sres0661.htm, as of 09.05.2012, 23:25.

http://www.faz.net/aktuell/finanzen/fonds-mehr/bestseller-autor-nassim-taleb-aus-kleinen-
fehlern-lernen-11745973.html, as of 10.05.2012, 23:27.

http://www.faz.net/aktuell/politik/ausland/japan-ein-fataler-sicherheitsmythos-
11829335.html, as of 23.07.2012, 16:32.

http://www.forbes.com/global2000/#p_1_s_a0_All%20industries_All%20countries_All%20st
ates, as of 20.07.2012, 11:38.

http://www.gpo.gov/fdsys/pkg/GPO-911REPORT/pdf/GPO-911REPORT.pdf, as of
24.03.2012, 13:48.

 http://www.iea.org/about/index.asp, as of 11.04.2012, 23:20.

http://www.iea.org/journalists/index.asp, as of 23.03.2012, 15:32.

http://www.iea.org/multimedia/videos_info.asp?filename=KISSINGER.flv, as of 11.04.2012,
23:46, starting from 0:44 minutes.

http://www.newsmax.com/Newsfront/AME-AMERICAME-ANNOTATED-
ASIA/2012/05/03/id/437974, as of 12.05.2012, 23:18.

http://www.nytimes.com/2007/04/22/books/chapters/0422-1st-tale.html?_r=1, as of
10.04.2012, 22:10.

http://www.nytimes.com/2007/04/22/books/chapters/0422-1st-tale.html?_r=2, as of
12.05.2012, 18:21.

http://www.pbs.org/wgbh/pages/frontline/shows/blackout/california/timeline.html, as of
14.07.2012, 12:03.

http://www.peri.umass.edu/fileadmin/pdf/Iraq3.pdf; as of 08.05.2012, 23:47.

http://www.sfgate.com/news/article/THE-ENERGY-CRUNCH-A-YEAR-LATER-State-s-
2834535.php, as of 13.07.2012, 15:51.

http://www.spiegel.de/spiegel/print/d-13501855.html, as of 09.05.2012, 23:56.

http://www.usatoday.com/news/index/iraq/nirq050.htm, as of 06.05.2012, 11:09.

http://www.wtrg.com/oil_graphs/PAPRPIQ.gif, as of 09.05.2012, 22:39.

http://www.wtrg.com/oil_graphs/PAPRPIR.gif, as of 09.05.2012, 22:50.

http://www-03.ibm.com/ibm/history/documents/pdf/faq.pdf, page 26, as of 24.03.2012, 13:03.

Office of Oil and Gas, Energy Information Administration: Oil Market Basics, chapter: Prices, http://www.eia.gov/pub/oil_gas/petroleum/analysis_publications/oil_market_basics/price_text.htm, as of 01.04.2012, 13:53.

Williams, Martyn: A legacy from the 1800s leaves Tokyo facing blackouts, http://www.itworld.com/business/140626/legacy-1800s-leaves-tokyo-facing-blackouts, as of 17.07.2012, 21:34.

7. Appendix

Table 1:

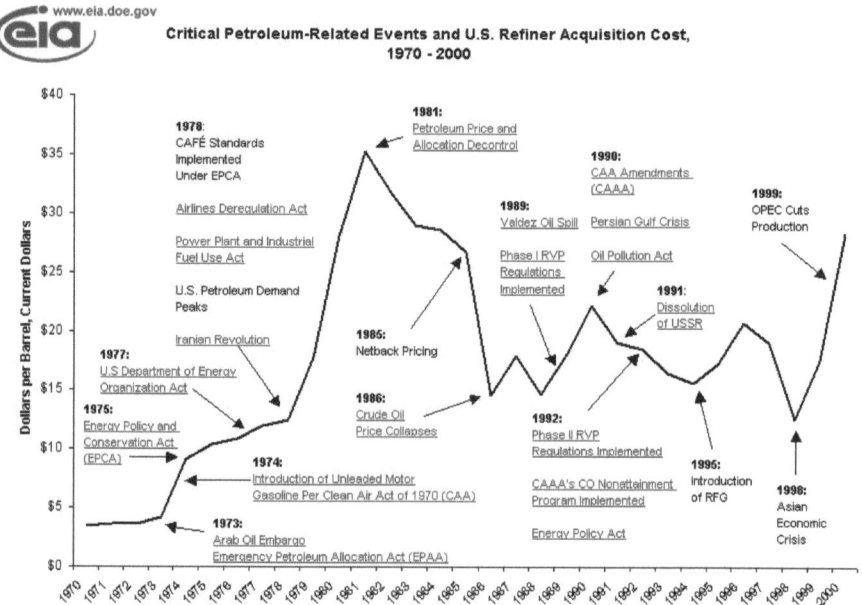

Source:

http://www.eia.gov/pub/oil_gas/petroleum/analysis_publications/chronology/petrochrohot graph.htm, as of 29.07.2012, 21:38.

Table 2:

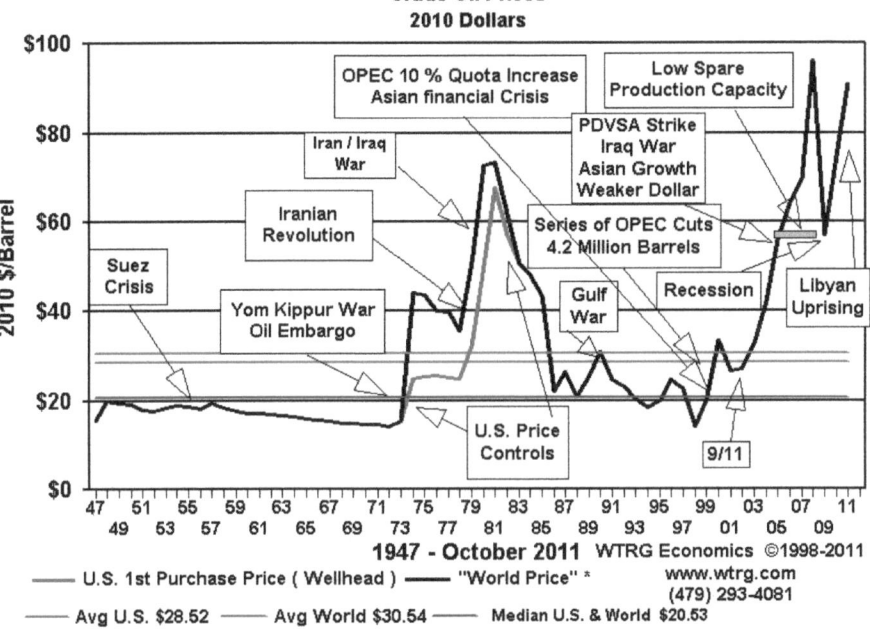

Source: http://www.wtrg.com/oil_graphs/oilprice1970.gif, as of 29.07.2012, 21:39.

Table 3:

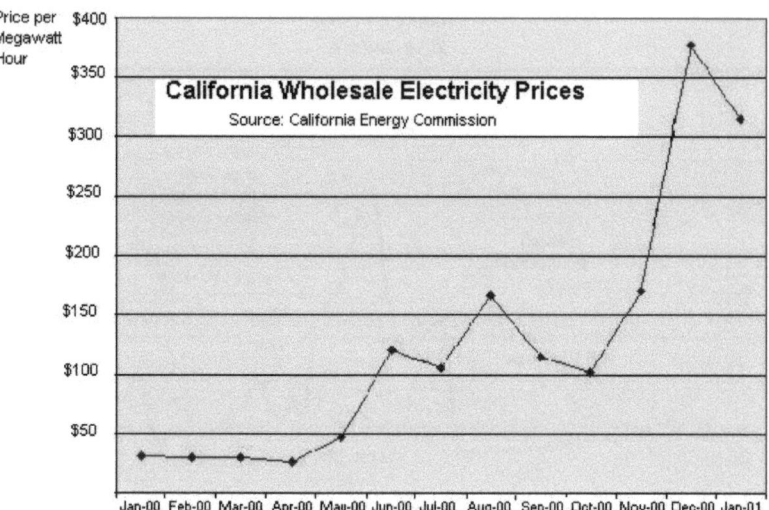

Source: http://1.bp.blogspot.com/-O8TfE5YKJAM/Tguyx-5oNsI/AAAAAAAAAsM/WqNG-FMhTlc/s1600/California%252BWholesale%252BElectricity%252BPrices.gif, as of 29.07.2012, 21:43.

Table 4:

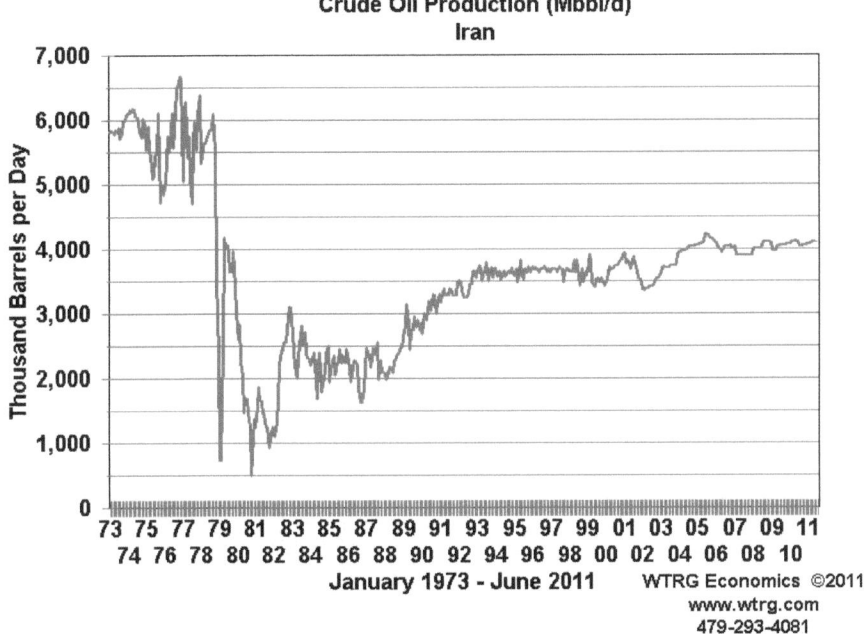

Source: http://www.wtrg.com/oil_graphs/PAPRPIR.gif, as of 29.07.2012, 22:22.